GRAMMAR

OF THE

MALABAR LANGUAGE

GRAMMAR

OF THE

MALABAR LANGUAGE,

BY

ROBERT DRUMMOND

GYAN

Published by

Gyan Publishing House
5, Ansari Road
Daryaganj, New Delhi-110002
Phone: 011-47034999, 9811692060
E-mail: books@gyanbooks.com

Distribution Network
gyanbooks.com
India, USA, Canada, UK, Australia, France

ISBN: 978-81-212-7328-2 (PB)
First Published, 1799

2nd Impression 2023

Printed at: Gyan Press, Delhi.

GRAMMAR OF THE MALABAR LANGUAGE
Author: ROBERT DRUMMOND

GRAMMAR

OF THE

MALABAR LANGUAGE,

BY

ROBERT DRUMMOND,

OF THE

Honorable East-India Company's

BOMBAY

MEDICAL ESTABLISHMENT.

Bombay:

PRINTED AT THE COURIER PRINTING OFFICE,

1799.

TO THE

Hon'ble JONATHAN DUNCAN,

Whose strenuous and unwearied exertions, in opposition to political prejudices and the mutual rancor of contending religious sects, equally intolerant in matters of faith and impatient of all legal restraint, have eminently contributed to the establishment of an enlightened system of jurisprudence in the province of Malabar, whereby the happiness of the people has been promoted, a state of the most atrocious licentiousness supplanted, and the permanent interests of an important appendage to the British Empire secured, the following work is humbly inscribed by

ROBERT DRUMMOND.

Bombay,
16th December, 1799.

PREFACE.

THE addition of territory acquired by the Honourable East India Company at the peace of Seringapatam in March 1792, by the cession of that part of the late Sultaun's possessions which lies on the Western side of the Sukhien or Ghaut Mountains, and extending from the Cavai River to Chetwa, since denominated the Province of Malabar, forms a new Era in the annals of the Presidency of Bombay. The theatre of its administration is extended over a considerable tract of territory parcelled out into a number of districts, of which each had its local chief previous to Hyder Ally Khan's conquest of the country in 1766. One of the first acts of the Hon'ble Company's Government was the re-establishment of these native Chieftains in their ancient family abodes; all of whom, at the commencement of the war before the last with Tippoo Sultaun, were either in a state of exile in the Travencore Country, or existing on the precarious means which occasional excursions from the impenetrable recesses of some parts of the country, afforded to them and their adherents.

The Rajas, Chief Nayrs, and other principal landholders, were from thence forward charged, on certain conditions, with the collection of the revenues of their respective districts on account of the Hon'ble Company; of which a liberal portion was alloted for their subsistence, as well as that of their families, and of their temples. To guard against the acts of oppression and extortion to which the rapacity of these local agents might expose the bulk of the inhabitants, it was found necessary to station a certain number of the Hon'ble Company's covenanted Servants in the districts, for the purpose of controling them in the exercise of their authority, so far as to prevent the husbandman from being deprived of that proportion of the fruits of his labour to which he was, under the new system, entitled.

The Collection of the customs, the superintendency of the mint, and the administration of justice, devolved exclusively and solely to the Company's servants, excepting in trials of a criminal nature which are conducted by a native judge; whose proceedings, altho' not under the control

of

of the British magistrate, are nevertheless subject to his remarks and animadversion, in cases where the native judge shall have deviated from the regulations laid down for his guidance. As an additional security to the lives of the people, his proceedings, which are held in the language of the country, are translated into English and transmitted in that form to the Chief Judge of the Province, for the execution of which office Commissioners have been appointed since May 1796, who confirm, mitigate, commute or annul the sentence, without having, in any case, the power to enhance it; or forward the trial to the Hon'ble the Governor in Council for the final determination of Government, according as the particular description of the case may, on reference to the Regulations, be found to require.

In fulfilling these important duties, in which the cause of humanity and the Company's interests, as well as those of individuals, are alike concerned, a proficiency in the language of Malabar is necessary to give full scope to the judicious and humane regulations framed for the administration of that Province, which secure to the various descriptions of the natives, their own respective laws, in all cases both Civil and Criminal, to a more extensive degree than the subsisting published Codes in other parts of our Indian territories. It was however soon found that our deficiency in this respect was but ill supplied by the interpreters which it was, at first, necessary to employ in the incessant intercourse between the Officers of Government, and the people of whose privileges and properties they were the guardians. This medium occasioned considerable unavoidable delay in all cases; and was often, in other respects, very unsatisfactory.

Many Gentlemen, both of the Civil and Military establishment, accordingly applied themselves to the study of the language. and several have made great progress. Five of these Gentlemen, Mr. *Hay Clephane* of the Civil service, Lieutenants *Joseph Watson* and *Hugh Stacey Osborne*, Mr. *James Wilson* Surgeon, and Mr. *John William Wye* Assistant Surgeon, on the Bombay establishment, are sufficiently masters of the language; and if the majority have not attained such a degree of perfection as is to be wished, it may be, in strict justice, imputed less to their want of zeal, than to the close application which the discharge of their current duties requires of them, and which leaves them little time for study. The supervenient disadvantage which all students have hitherto experienced, from the want of any introductory treatise on the structure of the language, has also not only retarded the progress of those who have engaged in this pursuit, but has appeared to many so insuperable an obstacle, as to deter them from the attempt.

Having, by surmounting these difficulties, acquired a sufficient knowledge of the language to excite a desire of improvement, I was happy in the opportunity of paying a visit to the Right Reverend *Luis*, the

titular

titular Bishop of *Uzula*, presiding over the Carmelite mission at Verapoly, in the vicinity of Cochin, in the month of April 1796, with whom I resided during the whole of the Monsoon, or rainy season, of that year. His long residence in that country, and the very high degree of respect in which he is deservedly considered by all classes of the natives, as well as Europeans, has enabled him to accumulate a fund of knowledge and learning in the Malabar language, which could not be easily attained in any other situation or circumstances.

The worthy Prelate's original object was the support and propagation of the Christian faith according to the tenets of the Church of Rome; but being entirely exempt from bigotry or prejudice of any kind, he, with a generosity equal to his hospitality, submited to me all his store of manuscripts, with an injunction to render them as subservient as possible to the end of diffusing a knowledge of the Malabar tongue, among the Hon'ble Company's representatives in their newly acquired possessions; whereby, he added, in the genuine spirit of philanthropy, the happiness and permanent interests of a numerous race of people who had been hitherto enslaved, would be more effectually secured to them under the mild and equitable institutes of a Christian Government.

Assisted by the instructions of my reverend host I prosecuted my favorite study, and formed the resolution of devoting my labors to the benefit of the public. These however would have been materially interrupted, if not entirely suspended, by subsequent ill health, if Mr. *Thomas Maurice Keate*, a Gentleman on the Civil establishment of Malabar, whose good offices claim my gratitude, while his virtues and talents attract my esteem and admiration, had not contributed his assistance in translating the manuscript, which was originally digested in the Latin tongue, in the same order in which the following English version is now presented. Mr. Keate, to a liberal European education, has also added, during his short stay in Malabar, no inconsiderable stock of the learning of that country; and I think I may without arrogance predict that, as this study is now become the principal pursuit of nearly all the Company's servants in Malabar, the business of that fine province will in a short time be conducted in the language of the natives, with great ease to the Gentlemen serving there, and dignity to their honorable employers.

I am authorized to draw this inference from the progressive state of peace, good order, and deference for the Officers of Government, which had become conspicuous, beyond all former example, for some time previous to my quitting the province in November last. My experience lately in the Office of Malabar translator to the Commissioners, contrasted with what passed under my observation, when acting in the same capacity under the Committee of Government, during the turbulent period of 1797, may I hope justify this remark on these unerring symp-

toms

P R E F A C E.

toms of ſubordination to the laws, and its concomitant ſecurity to perſons and property, produced in the ſhort ſpace of ſeven years, among a tumultuous race of Mohometans and Hindoos, bigots in religion and rivals in power, who had, for half a century before, ſpurned the one and diſregarded the other, with equal contumacy and wantonneſs.

Being compelled by bad health to relinquiſh, for the preſent, my profeſſional duties in this country I intended to commit the following ſheets to the preſs in England. On my late arrival in Bombay, however, I had the ſatisfaction to find a font of types, in the Malabar character, executed in an unexceptionable manner by Bheramjee Jeejebhoy, a Parſee inhabitant of this place, the ingenious artiſt who, without any other help or information than what he gleaned from Chambers's Dictionary of Arts and Sciences, ſucceeded in completing a font of Guzzeratty types a few years ago; and has, on this occaſion, again diſplayed his genius in a manner equally new and uſeful to ſociety in general, and to Government in particular, of which the ſubſequent work is a ſufficient teſtimony; and I preſume an apology for ſubjoining the following ſpecimen of his performance in the Guzzerat type is unneceſſary, altho' it has no connection with the preſent ſubject, further than to place, in a more conſpicuous point of view, the merits of the founder who has offered to the inhabitants of this part of India, the native claſs in particular, an eaſy and unexpected means of inſtruction.

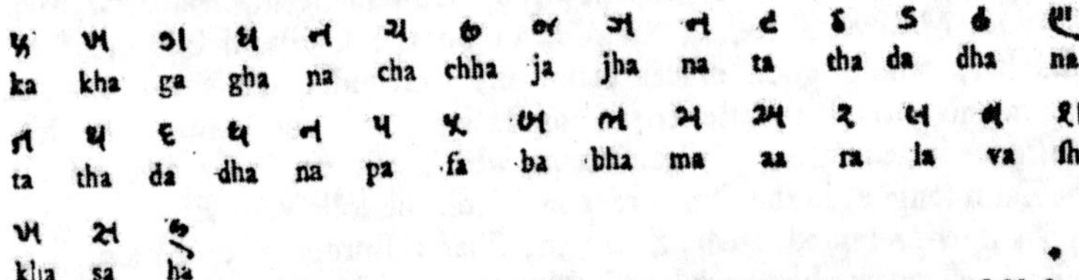

I now commit theſe Malabar rudiments to the public eye; and if they ſhall prove of ſufficient uſe to the learner to qualify him for diſcovering their imperfections, I ſhall think my time has been well employed. Their chief merit is the novelty of the attempt. I do not preſume to claim any other; nor do I advance any pretenſions to the talents which may be, hereafter, ſucceſsfully exerted in the improvement of this eſſay. I am not inſenſible to the teſtimonies of approbation which a few friends have beſtowed on it; but altho' my deference for their judgment, and my confidence in their ſincerity, will not, in juſtice to them, allow me to think my labour altogether loſt, I hope I may, without offence, be permitted, in ſympathy with my own feelings, to aſcribe to their partiality all the favor it may meet with.

ROBERT DRUMMOND.

Bombay,
16th December, 1799.

CONTENTS.

ALPHABET.

ALPHABET.

CHAPTER I.

THE Malabar language, as well as the Samſcradam or Sanſcrit, has fifty one Letters; ſixteen of which are vowels, the other thirty five are conſonants. The vocal letters are written in the following manner.

Character or figure.	*Name,*	*Power or Sound.*
അ	a	a ſhort
ആ	aá	á long
ഇ	i	i ſhort
ഈ	ii	i long
ഉ	u	u ſhort
ഊ	uú	ú long
ഋ	iru	ru ſhort
ൠ	iruu	rú long
ഌ	ilu	lu ſhort
ൡ	iluu	lú long
എ	e	é Engliſh ai
ഐ	ei	ei Diphtong
ഒ	o	o Diſtinct
ഔ	ow	ow as in own
അം	am	a & m
അഃ	ah	ah final aſpirate

Theſe

These are the ſixteen vowels, which may be called Initials, being only uſed by the Malabars under their preſent full ſhapes in the beginning of words, ſupplying their place with marks hereaſter to be explained; and now in their alphabetical order are ſhewn the thirty five ſimple, or radical conſonants following.

Figure,	*Name, and power*	*Figure,*	*Name, and power*
ക	ka	ധ	dha
ഖ	kha	ന	na
ഗ	ga	പ	pa
ഘ	ngha	ഫ	ippa
ങ	nga	ബ	ba
ച	cha	ഭ	bha
ഛ	ccha	മ	ma
ജ	ja	യ	ya
ഝ	inja	ര	ra
ഞ	nya	ല	la
ട	da	വ	va
ഠ	ta	ശ	ſha
ഡ	da	ഷ	iſha
ഢ	nda	സ	ſa
ണ	na	ഹ	ha
ത	ta	ള	la
ഥ	itta	ക്ഷ	kſha
ദ	da		

Malabar conſonants, as well ſimple as double, have the power of forming a ſyllable of themſelves, thus ന ല്ല ത nal-alda, good; മ ല a hill; whence it appears that, to pronounce the ſhort *a*, nothing is required to be added to the conſonant.

The

The long *a* is expreſſed by adding to the conſonant this figure ാ, which is called ദീർഘം dirgham; thus from പ, made പാ pa, comes പാവി *pavi* a ſinner; and from മ, comes മാ má or മാതാവ *madava*, ſignifying the mother.

This mark ി which is called *valli* വള്ളി, drawn over a conſonant, ſupplies the ſound of the ſhort *i*, whence from ല *la*, rendered into ലി *li*, you have ലിംഗം lingam, ſex; or with the antecedent name of the Heathen God ശിവലിംഗം *ſhiva lingam*, from ബ *ba* changed into ബി bi, is made ബിംബം *bimbam* an Idol, Image, or ſtatue, and it is only neceſſary to make the ſame curved ſtroke with a circle in the forepart, thus to ീ, expreſs the long vowel ഈ *i*, as from മ, changed into മീ, with the addition of ൻ *n*, is written the monoſyllable മീൻ *min*, fiſh.

In writing however the ſhort *u*, and long vowel *u* there are various modes which may be reduced to the following rules.

To the conſonants ക *k*, and ര *r*, are added theſe marks ു and ൂ, thus from ക made കു ku, and കൂ *ku*, comes കുംഭം *kumbham* aquarius, and കൂൻ *kun* a hump; from ര made രു *ru* comes രുദ്രൻ *Rudren* a name for Viſhnu, and from രൂ *ru* long comes രൂപം *rubam*, an Image, or picture. It may be as well however to draw the ſign of the *u* long from the left to the right, thus ൂ added to ര, as in അരുളിച്ചെയ്തു aruli *Cheyadu*, the Raja ordered.

The

The *u* ſhort and *u* long, are expreſſed at the end of గ చ జ ట భ ష హ by adding to theſe conſonants the marks ు and ూ reſpectively; inſtance గ *ga* made గు *gu*, and గూ *gù*,

చ	icha	చు	ichu	చూ	ichú
జ	ja	జు	ju	జూ	jú
ట	ta	టు	tu	టూ	tú
భ	bha	భు	bhu	భూ	bhú
ష	ſha	షు	ſhu	షూ	ſhú
హ	ha	హు	hu	హూ	hú

The letters ణ *na*, and న *na*, and their compounds, ణ్ణ and న్న *nna* take the figures of ſhort and long *u* in this way ణు *nu*, ణూ nu, ను *nu*, నూ *nú*.

ణ్ణు ణ్ణూ న్ను న్నూ

Theſe two marks for ſhort and long *u* viz. ు ూ are joined to the bottom of the remaining conſonants;

Thus ల *la* makes లు *lu*, లూ *lú* చ *cha* చు *chu* చూ *chú* ప *pa* పు *pú* పూ *pu* and ſo on the reſt, as may be ſeen under the next head of conſonants compound, or joined with vowels.

Theſe figures ృ and ౄ, drawn down from the right, with a gentle curvature returning from the left, expreſs the vowels ఋ and ౠ *iru*, and *iru* ſhort, and long, as from స *sa*, comes సృ *ſru* సౄ *ſru*.

మ	ma	మృ	miru,	మౄ	mirú
క	ka	కృ	kiru,	కౄ	kirú

ſum.

Sometimes, however, the letter ക *ka* expreſſes the *ru* ſhort; in this manner, കൃ *kru*, whence കൃപ *kruva*, mercy; കൃമി *krumi* a worm; കൃഷ്ണ *kraſhna* an Incarnate of Viſhnu. Let it be obſerved that the ſound of the *i* is ſcarcely in ſpeech before this character which is generally pronounced *ra* ſhort. The vowels ഌ *ilu*, and ൡ ilu follow the conſonant entire as ചഌ, *chilu* ചൡ chilu; But ſeldom occur in Malabar writings.

They expreſs the vowel എ e by this mark െ, which is called പുള്ളി *pulli*, and is always, placed before the conſonant thus from ക *ka* is, കെ ke, as കെഴക്ക *keryaka* Eaſt, മ *ma* മെ me, and മെഘം *megam* a cloud, and this mark or *pulli* is doubled before a conſonant in place of the diphthong ഐ, thus െ െ placed before മ *ma* makes മൈ *mei* the body. ക *ka* കൈ *kei* or *kai* the hand.

They ſignify ഒ *o* by putting the conſonant between theſe two figures െ and ാ, thus from മ *ma*, comes മൊ *mo*, മൊല്ല *molla* the boſoms, and മൊള *mola* a bamboo, and മൊളക *molaga*, pepper.

They figure the Diphthong ഔ *ow* by theſe two marks െ and ൗ placing the conſonant between them, ſo പ *pa*, becomes പൌ pow, പൌരുഷം *powruſham* pride, Pompoſity. The ſingle addition of ൗ however, not unfrequently expreſſes the Diphthong added to a conſonant thus സ *sa*, സൗ *sow*, സൗഖ്യം *ſaw hyam* happineſs, comfort.

അം or അം *am* is added to conſonants entire as രം ram ഠം odam.

The aſpirate vow അഃ is expreſſed by placing the two circles, which are called വിസർഗ്ഗം *viſarggam*, at the end of whatever conſonant.

CHAPTER II.

CHAPTER II.

Shewing the radical consonants with the vowels joined, and forming the first natural, or simple syllables

ക കാ കി കീ കു കൂ കൃ കൄ കഌ കൡ കെ കൈ കൊ കൌ കം കഃ

ka, ka, ki, ki, ku, ku, kru, kru, kilu, kilu, ka, kei, ko, kow, kam, ka.

ഖ ഖാ ഖി ഖീ ഖു ഖൂ ഖൃ ഖൄ ഖഌ ഖൡ ഖെ ഖൈ ഖൊ ഖൌ ഖം ഖഃ

ഗ ഗാ ഗി ഗീ ഗു ഗൂ ഗൃ ഗൄ ഗഌ ഗൡ ഗെ ഗൈ ഗൊ ഗൌ ഗം ഗഃ

ഘ ഘാ ഘി ഘീ ഘു ഘൂ ഘൃ ഘൄ ഘഌ ഘൡ ഘെ ഘൈ ഘൊ ഘൌ ഘം ഘഃ

ങ ങാ ങി ങീ ങു ങൂ ങൃ ങൄ ങഌ ങൡ ങെ ങൈ ങൊ ങൌ ങം ങഃ

ച ചാ ചി ചീ ചു ചൂ ചൃ ചൄ ചഌ ചൡ ചെ ചൈ ചൊ ചൌ ചം ചഃ

ഛ ഛാ ഛി ഛീ ഛു ഛൂ ഛൃ ഛൄ ഛഌ ഛൡ ഛെ ഛൈ ഛൊ ഛൌ ഛം ഛഃ

ജ ജാ ജി ജീ ജു ജൂ ജൃ ജൄ ജഌ ജൡ ജെ ജൈ ജൊ ജൌ ജം ജഃ

ഝ ഝാ ഝി ഝീ ഝു ഝൂ ഝൃ ഝൄ ഝഌ ഝൡ ഝെ ഝൈ ഝൊ ഝൌ ഝം ഝഃ

ഞ ഞാ ഞി ഞീ ഞു ഞൂ ഞൃ ഞൄ ഞഌ ഞൡ ഞെ ഞൈ ഞൊ ഞൌ ഞം ഞഃ

ട ടാ ടി ടീ ടു ടൂ ടൃ ടൄ ടഌ ടൡ ടെ ടൈ ടൊ ടൌ ടം ടഃ

ഠ

ഠ ഠാ ഠി ഠീ ഠു ഠൂ ഠൃ ഠൄ ഠൢ ഠൣ ഠെ ഠൈ ഠൊ ഠൌ ഠം ഠഃ

ഡ ഡാ ഡി ഡീ ഡു ഡൂ ഡൃ ഡൄ ഡൢ ഡൣ ഡെ ഡൈ ഡൊ ഡൌ ഡം ഡഃ

ഢ ഢാ ഢി ഢീ ഢു ഢൂ ഢൃ ഢൄ ഢൢ ഢൣ ഢെ ഢൈ ഢൊ ഢൌ ഢം ഢഃ

ണ ണാ ണി ണീ ണു ണൂ ണൃ ണൄ ണൢ ണൣ ണെ ണൈ ണൊ ണൌ ണം ണഃ

ത താ തി തീ തു തൂ തൃ തൄ തൢ തൣ തെ തൈ തൊ തൌ തം തഃ

ഥ ഥാ ഥി ഥീ ഥു ഥൂ ഥൃ ഥൄ ഥൢ ഥൣ ഥെ ഥൈ ഥൊ ഥൌ ഥം ഥഃ

ദ ദാ ദി ദീ ദു ദൂ ദൃ ദൄ ദൢ ദൣ ദെ ദൈ ദൊ ദൌ ദം ദഃ

ധ ധാ ധി ധീ ധു ധൂ ധൃ ധൄ ധൢ ധൣ ധെ ധൈ ധൊ ധൌ ധം ധഃ

ന നാ നി നീ നു നൂ നൃ നൄ നൢ നൣ നെ നൈ നൊ നൌ നം നഃ

പ പാ പി പീ പു പൂ പൃ പൄ പൢ പൣ പെ പൈ പൊ പൌ പം പഃ

ഫ ഫാ ഫി ഫീ ഫു ഫൂ ഫൃ ഫൄ ഫൢ ഫൣ ഫെ ഫൈ ഫൊ ഫൌ ഫം ഫഃ

ബ ബാ ബി ബീ ബു ബൂ ബൃ ബൄ ബൢ ബൣ ബെ ബൈ ബൊ ബൌ ബം ബഃ

ഭ ഭാ ഭി ഭീ ഭു ഭൂ ഭൃ ഭൄ ഭൢ ഭൣ ഭെ ഭൈ ഭൊ ഭൌ ഭം ഭഃ

മ മാ മി മീ മു മൂ മൃ മൄ മൢ മൣ മെ മൈ മൊ മൌ മം മഃ

യ യാ യി യീ യു യൂ യൃ യൄ യൢ യൣ യെ യൈ യൊ യൌ യം യഃ

ര രാ രി രീ രു രൂ രൃ രൄ രൢ രൣ രെ രൈ രൊ രൌ രം രഃ

ല ലാ ലി ലീ ലു ലൂ ലൃ ലൄ ലൢ ലൣ ലെ ലൈ ലൊ ലൌ ലം ലഃ
വ വാ വി വീ വു വൂ വൃ വൄ വൢ വൣ വെ വൈ വൊ വൌ വം വഃ
ശ ശാ ശി ശീ ശു ശൂ ശൃ ശൄ ശൢ ശൣ ശെ ശൈ ശൊ ശൌ ശം ശഃ
ഷ ഷാ ഷി ഷീ ഷു ഷൂ ഷൃ ഷൄ ഷൢ ഷൣ ഷെ ഷൈ ഷൊ ഷൌ ഷം ഷഃ
സ സാ സി സീ സു സൂ സൃ സൄ സൢ സൣ സെ സൈ സൊ സൌ സം സഃ
ഹ ഹാ ഹി ഹീ ഹു ഹൂ ഹൃ ഹൄ ഹൢ ഹൣ ഹെ ഹൈ ഹൊ ഹൌ ഹം ഹഃ
ള ളാ ളി ളീ ളു ളൂ ളൃ ളൄ ളൢ ളൣ ളെ ളൈ ളൊ ളൌ ളം ളഃ
ക്ഷ ക്ഷാ ക്ഷി ക്ഷീ ക്ഷു ക്ഷൂ ക്ഷൃ ക്ഷൄ ക്ഷൢ ക്ഷൣ ക്ഷെ ക്ഷൈ ക്ഷൊ ക്ഷൌ ക്ഷം ക്ഷഃ

CHAPTER III.

CHAPTER III.

Of double and triple compound Conſonants.

After thus demonſtrating the radical letters, and plain ſyllables the Malabars teach the further characters compoſed of two, or three conſonants, which they term പൂൎണ്ണാക്ഷരം *Purnakſharam*, and as they exhibit them in five claſses they are ſo divided here.

CLASS FIRST.

Contains the conſonants to which is coupled this figure ്യ brought from the tail of the letter, and under it to the left, and carried back beyond its right whence it commenced; the pronounciation reſembles the *iota* of the Greeks, but the English conſonantal *y* ſounds it very well, making a light inspiration on, and gently expreſſing the preceding letter.

ക്യ ഖ്യ ഗ്യ ഘ്യ ങ്യ ച്യ ഛ്യ ജ്യ ഝ്യ ഞ്യ ട്യ
ഠ്യ ഡ്യ ഢ്യ ണ്യ ത്യ ഥ്യ ദ്യ ധ്യ ന്യ പ്യ ഫ്യ
ബ്യ ഭ്യ മ്യ യ്യ ര്യ ല്യ വ്യ ശ്യ ഷ്യ സ്യ ഹ്യ
ള്യ ക്ഷ്യ. i. e. *kya*, and ſo forth.

This form of compounds ſeldom occurs in the beginning of words, but in the middle, or end, E. G. സത്യം *ſatyam*, കല്യാണം *kalyanam*, മൃത്യം *murtyam*, Truth, marriage, Death.

To theſe letters may be added the figures which diſtinguiſh the vowels, in this manner ക്യാ kya, ക്യോ kyo, ക്യെ kye, &c.

CLASS

CLASS SECOND.

In this class are enumerated the consonants to which *ra* is added, and which is done by this figure ◡ drawn from the right to the left of the consonant, which is then deprived of the vocal sound that it bears in its radical, or simple shape thus క *ka* is rendered క్ర *kra*, and so on, as under.

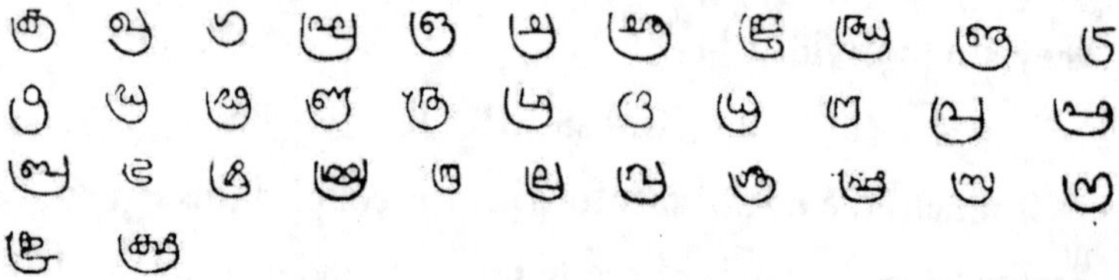

All these may have the figures denoting the vowels tied to them, as in క్రియ *kriya* sacrifice, క్రూరిన్ *krurin* a cruel-man.

CLASS THIRD

Embraces those consonants to which this letter, ల *la*, is subjoined, as క్ల *kla* &c.

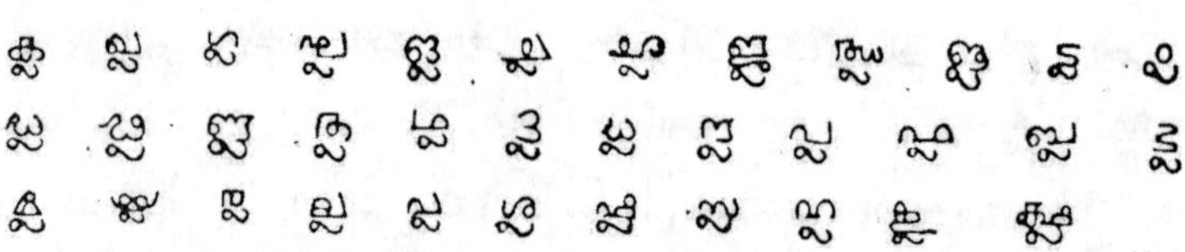

These letters are also united with vowels, as ప్లా *pla*, ప్లి *pli*, ప్లు *plu*.

CLASS FOURTH.

This exhibits those consonants which carry on their back the figure ‿, being a contraction of the letter వ *va* and to be be brought out as we pronounce *wa*, the first syllable in water, so ക്വ *kwa* &c.

ക്വ ഖ്വ ഗ്വ ഘ്വ ങ്വ ച്വ ഛ്വ ജ്വ ഝ്വ ഞ്വ
ട്വ ഠ്വ ഡ്വ ഢ്വ ണ്വ ത്വ ഥ്വ ദ്വ ധ്വ ന്വ പ്വ
ഫ്വ ബ്വ ഭ്വ മ്വ യ്വ ര്വ ല്വ വ്വ ശ്വ ഷ്വ
സ്വ ഹ്വ ള്വ ക്ഷ്വ

CLASS FIFTH.

The last class of Compound consonants is marked by this slight stroke, which has the sound of *r* before the consonant, over which it is affixed, as in തൎക്കം *tarkam*, Disputation.

ൎക ൎഖ ൎഗ ൎഘ ൎങ ൎച ൎഛ ൎജ ൎഝ ൎഞ ൎട ൎഠ ൎഡ
ൎഢ ൎണ ൎത ൎഥ ൎദ ൎധ ൎന ൎപ ൎഫ ൎബ ൎഭ ൎമ ൎയ
ൎര ൎല ൎവ ൎശ ൎഷ ൎസ ൎഹ ൎള ൎക്ഷ

To these may be joined; or added all the figures of the vowels that are necessary in speech.

CHAPTER IV.

Here follow the fifth order of letters where the Malabars make another form of double consonants, and, in this table, these are exhibited with the five short natural vowels *a e i o u*, in their native order.

	a	*i*	*u*	*e*	*o*
kka	ക്ക	ക്കി	ക്കു	ക്കെ	ക്കൊ
nka	ങ്ക	ങ്കി	ങ്കു	ങ്കെ	ങ്കൊ
nga	ങ്ങ	ങ്ങി	ങ്ങു	ങ്ങെ	ങ്ങൊ

ccha

ccha	ച്ച	ച്ചി	ച്ചു	ച്ചെ	ച്ചൌ
njja	ഞ്ജ	ഞ്ജി	ഞ്ജു	ഞ്ജെ	ഞ്ജൌ
nnya	ഞ്ഞ	ഞ്ഞി	ഞ്ഞു	ഞ്ഞെ	ഞ്ഞൌ
tta	ട്ട	ട്ടി	ട്ടു	ട്ടെ	ട്ടൌ
nda	ണ്ട	ണ്ടി	ണ്ടു	ണ്ടെ	ണ്ടൌ
nna	ണ്ണ	ണ്ണി	ണ്ണു	ണ്ണെ	ണ്ണൌ
tta	ത്ത	ത്തി	ത്തു	ത്തെ	ത്തൌ
nta	ന്ത	ന്തി	ന്തു	ന്തെ	ന്തൌ
nna	ന്ന	ന്നി	ന്നു	ന്നെ	ന്നൌ
ppa	പ്പ	പ്പി	പ്പു	പ്പെ	പ്പൌ
mpa	മ്പ	മ്പി	മ്പു	മ്പെ	മ്പൌ
mma	മ്മ	മ്മി	മ്മു	മ്മെ	മ്മൌ
iya	യ്യ	യ്യി	യ്യു	യ്യെ	യ്യൌ
tta	റ്റ	റ്റി	റ്റു	റ്റെ	റ്റൌ
nta	ന്റ	ന്റി	ന്റു	ന്റെ	ന്റൌ
lla	ല്ല	ല്ലി	ല്ലു	ല്ലെ	ല്ലൌ
uva	വ്വ	വ്വി	വ്വു	വ്വെ	വ്വൌ
ſſha	ശ്ശ	ശ്ശി	ശ്ശു	ശ്ശെ	ശ്ശൌ
ſhta	ഷ്ട	ഷ്ടി	ഷ്ടു	ഷ്ടെ	ഷ്ടൌ
ſſa	സ്സ	സ്സി	സ്സു	സ്സെ	സ്സൌ
hha	ഹ്ഹ	ഹ്ഹി	ഹ്ഹു	ഹ്ഹെ	ഹ്ഹൌ
lla	ള്ള	ള്ളി	ള്ളു	ള്ളെ	ള്ളൌ
kſhma	ക്ഷ്മ	ക്ഷ്മി	ക്ഷ്മു	ക്ഷ്മെ	ക്ഷ്മൌ

For the pronounciation of the above examples; ſee the orthography at the end of the Grammar, as well as for the following

lowing five finals.

ൺ ൻ ർ ൽ ൾ

Which can only be attained with experience in conversation, as may be said, of the letters ര്യ *rya* (the *y* scarcely sounded), and റ *ra*, which are much in use, tho' left out of the Malabar alphabet.

With a knowledge of the preceding examples, the various other connections may be readily understood, and this science is called by the teachers അക്ഷരക്കെട്ട *akshaketta*, or compling, and tying of letters as ക്തി *kti* ഗ്നി *gni*, ക്ഷ്മി *kshmi* in ശക്തി *shakti*, അഗ്നി *agni*, and ലക്ഷ്മി *Lakshmi* signifying Strength, Fire and *Lakshmi* the Goddess of corn which will serve for example, and സ്ത്രീ *stri* a woman to which may be added some hundreds, yea thounsands more.

TABLE OF NUMERAL MARKS.

Figure,	*Name*	*Pronounce,*	*N.*
൧	ഒന്ന	Onna	1
൨	രണ്ട	Randa	2
൩	മൂന	Muna	3
൪	നാല	Nala	4
൫	അഞ്ച	Anja	5
൬	ആറ	Ara	6
൭	ഏഴ	Era	7
൮	എട്ട	Eta	8

൯

Figure,	*Name,*	*Pronounce,*	*N.*
൯	ഒമ്പത	Onbada	9
൰	പത്ത	Patta	10
൰൧	പതിനൊന്ന	Padinonna	11
൰൨	പന്ത്രണ്ട	Pandaranda	12
൰൩	പതിമൂന്ന	Padimuna	13
൰൪	പതിനാല	padinala	14
൰൫	പതിനഞ്ച	Padinanja	15
൰൬	പതിനാറ	Padinara	16
൰൭	പതിനേഴ	Padinera	17
൰൮	പതിനെട്ട	Padineta	18
൰൯	പത്തൊമ്പത	Patt,onbada	16
൨൰	ഇരുപത	Irivada	20
൨൰൧	ഇരുപത്തൊന്ന	Irivattonna	21
൨൰൨	ഇരുപത്തിരണ്ട	Irivattaranda	22
൨൰൩	ഇരുപത്തിമൂന്ന	Irivattamuna	23
൨൰൪	ഇരുപത്തിനാല	Irivattanala	24
൨൰൫	ഇരുപത്തഞ്ച	Irivattanja	25
൨൰൬	ഇരുപത്താറ	Irivattara	26
൨൰൭	ഇരുപത്തേഴ	Irivattera	27
൨൰൮	ഇരുപത്തെട്ട	Irivatteta	28
൨൰൯	ഇരുപത്തൊമ്പത	Irivattonbada	29
൩൰	മുപ്പത	Muppada	30
൪൰	നാല്പത	Nalpada	40
൫൰	അമ്പത	Anbada	50

Figure,	*Name,*	*Pronounce,*	*N.*
൬൰	ആറുപത	Aravadr	60
൭൰	എഴുപത	Eluʌvda	70
൮൰	എമ്പത	Enbada	80
൯൰	തൊണ്ണൂറ	Tonnura	90
൱	നൂറ	Nura	100
൱൰	നൂററൊരുവത	Nutoruvada	110
൨൱	ഇരുനൂറ	Irunuta	209
൩൱	മുന്നൂറ	Munura	300
൪൱	നാനൂറ	Nanura	400
൫൱	അഞ്ഞൂറ	Anyura	500
൬൱	ആറുനൂറ	Aranura	600
൭൱	എഴുനൂറ	Elanura	700
൮൱	എണ്ണൂറ	Eunura	800
൯൱	തൊള്ളായിരം	Tolluiram	900
൲	ആയിരം	Airam	1000
൧൲	ഒരായിരം	Orairam	1000
൰൲	പതിനായിരം	Padinairam	10,000
൨൰൲	ഇരുവതിനായിരം	Irivadinairam	20,000
൱൲	നൂറായിരം	Nuraıram	100,000
൰൱൲	പത്തനൂറായിരം	PattaNurairam	1000,000
൨൰൱൲	ഇരുവതനൂറായിരം	IrivadaNurairam	2000,000
൱൱൲	നൂറനൂറായിരം	NuraNurairam	10,000,000
൧൱൲	ലക്ഷം	Lakſhum, a Lack	100,000
൰൱൲	പത്തലക്ഷം	Pattalakſhum, 10 lacks	10,00,000

നൂറല

നൂറലക്ഷത്തിനൊരുകോടി *Nura Lakſhatiua ora kody*, For a hundred Lacks there is a kody or, - - 10,000,000

To make the ordinal numbers it is only neceſſary to add ാം *am*, for the maſculine, and feminine (or when adjectively placed before Subſtantives to the conſonants terminating with a vocal ſound) and ാമത for the neuter, or in an adverbial ſenſe, as more fully explained in the 4 th ſection of Lecture 2. d, thus, maſc. ഒന്നാം *onam*, Feme. ഒന്നാമ ഒന്നാമത *onnamata* the firſt, but when the numeral terminates in ം *m*, as in ആയിരം *airum* a thouſand, the final ം *m* is changed into ത്ത *tt* and ാം *am* added; thus ആയിരത്താം, ാമത *airattam*, *amatta* the thouſandth.

LECTURE

LECTURE FIRST.

OF THE DECLENSION OF SUBSTANTIVES.

All nouns substantive in the Malabar language may be referred to two forms of declension; to the first of which belong all nouns ending in *a* short, or in ൽ, or ൾ, in ൻ, in ൺ, or in ർ; that is, in al, el, il, ol, ul; or an, en, in, on, un, or in ar, er, ir, &c.

To the second belong all nouns in *a* long, or in *i*.

Nouns of the first declension in *a* short, (that is in any letter which I call a vocal consonant) form the genitive by changing *a* into *i* and adding thereto ന്റെ; the dative by adding ന; the accusative നെ and the vocative by changing *a* into *e*; the first ablative (of which this language has four) by adding ൽ to the termination of the nominative already changed in the oblique case into *i*; this ablative signifies *in*; to make the second നോട is added, which answers to our sign of the ablative *with*; the third ends in നാൽ having the power of, by, or through the means of; the last ablative is formed by adding the particle നിന്ന to the first, thus യിൽനിന്ന and means, from or out of.–ex. gr.

Singular,		*Plural.*	
Nom.	വില്ല a bow.	Nom.	വില്ലുകൾ
Gen.	വില്ലിന്റെ	Gen.	വില്ലുകളുടെ
Dat.	വില്ലിന	Dat.	വില്ലുകൾക്ക

Acc.

Singular,		*Plural.*	
Acc.	വില്ലിനെ	Acc.	വില്ലുകളെ
Voc.	വില്ലെ	Voc.	the ſame
1ſt abl.	വില്ലിൽ	1ſt abl.	വില്ലുകളിൽനിന്ന
2d.	വില്ലിനോട	2d.	വില്ലുകളോട
3d.	വില്ലിനാൽ	3d.	വില്ലുകളാൽ
4th.	വില്ലിൽനിന്ന	4th.	വില്ലുകളിൽനിന്ന

The caſes of the plural number are formed by changing the final *a* of the ſingular, into *u* ſhort; and adding കൾ as the above example ſheweth.

Such is always the form of the plural in words ſignifying irrational objects; but the names of reaſonable beings reject the *a*, or final letter, adding inſtead thereof the termination കൾ in the nominative plural, or കന്മാർ. Ex. gr. കർത്താവ a Lord makes കർത്താക്കൾ or കർത്താക്കന്മാർ; Gen. കർത്താക്കളുടെ. കർത്താക്കന്മാരുടെ. In the ſame manner are declined the following words രാജാവ a King, പിതാവ a Father, മാതാവ Mother, ഭ്രാതാവ a Brother; and ſome other words derived from the Sanſcrit.

To the ſame form of declenſion are referred all nouns ending in ട or റ, with this partial difference that, in the oblique caſe, they double this letter in the ſingular into ട്ട or റ്റ except in the vocative. For inſtance വീട a houſe, makes in the genitive വീട്ടിന്റെ, and not വീടിന്റെ. ആറ; a River is not written ആറിന്റെ in the genitive, but ആറ്റിന്റെ; the

the face മുകറ gen. മുകററിന്റെ; പയറ a Bean; കയറ rope, ആട a sheep, and others in the same manner which make the vocative like വില്ലെ, except വീട, which makes വീടെ and ആറെ. In the plural these nouns are declined precisely like വില്ലുകൾ as before cited, thus വീടുകൾ houses; Gen. വീടുകളുടെ; ആറുകൾ Rivers &c.

We proceed to nouns ending in al, el, il, ol, ul. These all change the final ൽ or ൾ into ലി or ളി respectively, and are then declined as in the former Examples വില്ലെ &c. Thus ആൾ a person, in the gen. ആളിന്റെ; കാൽ the Foot gen; കാലിന്റെ. വിരൽ the Finger, വിരലിന്റെ. എച്ചിൽ the refuse of a meal, എച്ചിലിന്റെ. താക്കോൽ key, താക്കോലിന്റെ. പൊരുൾ Exposition, പൊരുളിന്റെ.

In the plural ൽ is changed into ല്ല and ൾ into ള്ള, and the cases are formed as in വില്ലുകൾ; thus ആള്ളുകൾ persons, ആള്ളുകളുടെ; കാല്ലുകൾ feet, gen. കാല്ലുകളുടെ.

The following are exceptions from the general rule ചെക്കൻ a boy, ആണ a male, പെണ്ണ a female, കിടാവ a young man, പുണ്യം sanctity, ഭാഗ്യം blessedness, ഗ്രഹം a planet, നക്ഷത്രം a star, മേഘം a cloud, and others which do not make ചെക്കല്ലുകൾ but ചെക്കങ്ങൾ, and in like manner the rest.

But the two following nouns മകൾ a Daughter, and മരുമകൾ a Niece are declined in the singular number like വില്ലുകൾ; thus മകൾ gen മകളുടെ; dat മകൾക്കു; മരുമകൾ

a Niece, gen മരുമകളുടെ; dat മരുമകൾക്കു; in the plural they end in ഉകൾ, as കർത്താവുകൾ and cther nouus ending in wa വ or va.

We come now to nouns ending in ൻ which belong to the first declension, but since they differ from each other, according to the preceding vowel, whether an, en, in, on, un, be the termination, they require to be separately considered.

Nouns then ending with *an* are declined in the singular like പിള്ള; with this difference that they retain the final *an*, and add thereto ടെ in this manner ന്റെ; thus തമ്പുരാൻ a God or King, does not make the genitive തമ്പുരാവിന്റെ, but തമ്പുരാന്റെ; in the dative ൻ is changed into ന as തമ്പുരാന; in the acc. and voc. into നെ making തമ്പുരാനെ; in the ablatives ൻ is changed into നാൽ. നോട. ന്നാൽ and നിൽനിന്നു, thus തമ്പുരാനാൽ. തമ്പുരാനോട. തമ്പുരാന്നാൽ. തമ്പുരാനിൽനിന്നു. and others in the same manner.

But the plural of these nouns is commonly made by adding to the final letter the particle മാർ, and is varied as in പുത്രന്മാർ sons, in a subsequent example, gen, പുത്രന്മാരുടെ; thus from പിശാചൻ a demon, comes in the gen. പിശാചന്മാരുടെ; dat. പിശാചന്മാൎക്കു, from തട്ടാൻ a Goldsmith is formed തട്ടാന്മാരുടെ.

Sometimes however, tho' not frequently, these nouns change

change ൻ into ർ in the plural, thus അടിയാൻ a tean, makes അടിയാർ, അടിയാരുടെ, അടിയാൎക്കു and so on like പുത്രൻ; but observe കൎത്താവൻ is the only word of this termination which makes in the plural, either കൎത്താവാക്കൾ, or കൎത്താക്കന്മാർ, like what has been before observed of മാതാവു, കൎത്താവു.

Nouns ending in *en* are declined like the former example കൎത്താവൻ, that is by adding in the genitive ന്റെ in the dative ന &c. thus പുത്രൻ a son, gen. പുത്രന്റെ, dat. പുത്രന, acc. പുത്രനെ, voc. പുത്രാ, 1st abl. പുത്രനാൽ, 2d, പുത്രനോട, 3d, പുത്രനാലെ, 4th, പുത്രനിങ്കൽ, thus are all nouns ending in *en* declined in the singular.

Observe that these nouns usually form the voc. by changing ൻ into *a* long ാ as പുത്രാ, o son, തമ്പുരാൻ a lord or chief തമ്പുരാ, അപ്പൻ a father, അപ്പാ o father.

Except മകൻ a son, and മരുമകൻ a nephew, which make the vocative മകനെ and മരുമകനെ; other exceptions are തേൻ honey, and some other names of irrational things, which change ൻ into ന, and are declined like വി ള thus തേനിന്റെ of honey, dat. തേനിന്ന. പേൻ a louse makes പേനിന്റെ, dat. പേനിന്ന &c. They have however no plural; which is indeed the case with almost all irrationals, in which the singular is used for the plural.

Nouns of this termination form the plural by adding മാർ to

to the final ൻ, or by changing this latter into ർ, as was above noticed in speaking of nouns in *an*, thus പുത്രർ or പുത്രന്മാർ sons, പുത്രരുടെ or പുത്രന്മാരുടെ of sons, പുത്രർക്കു or പുത്രന്മാർക്കു to sons, പുത്രരെ or പുത്രന്മാരെ in the acc. and voc. പുത്രരാൽ or പുത്രന്മാരാൽ, പുത്രരോടു or പുത്രന്മാരോടു. പുത്രരാലെ or പുത്രന്മാരാലെ. പുത്രരിൽനിന്നു or പുത്രന്മാരിൽനിന്നു in the ablatives respectively.

There are however some nouns which I should rather have മാർ than ർ, as from ബന്ധുവൻ, a kinsman, it is not proper to say in the plural ബന്ധുവർ, but ബന്ധുവന്മാർ, ജ്യേഷ്ഠൻ, ജ്യേഷ്ഠന്മാർ senior brothers, but these refinements can only be learnt from practice.

The following are exceptions from the general Rule; കിടാത്തൻ a boy, which makes കിടാങ്ങൾ and is declined, like ഏറുകാരങ്ങൾ hereafter to be cited, മകൻ a son, and മരുമകൻ a Nephew, make the plural മക്കൾ, and മരുമക്കൾ and are declined like പശുക്കൾ, and other nouns in *u* which will be hereafter explained.

Nouns ending in ഈൻ change the final ൻ into ന and are declined like വിള; thus മീൻ fish makes മീനിന്റെ. തീൻ food തീനിന്റെ.

Nouns in *on* are declined like those in *an*, by making the genitive to end in ന്റെ, and changing the dative into ന്നു, as

മന

മഹറോൻ Excommunication, മഹറോനെന്റെ. ശലൊമൊൻ Salomon ശലൊമൊനെന്റെ &c.

Nouns ending in *un* are declined like വില്ല changing ൺ into ണി; for example കൂൺ a humpback കൂണിന്റെ. തൂൺ a Pillar തൂണിന്റെ.

Except നാത്തൂൻ a female relation which makes നാത്തൂന്റെ, and in the plural നാത്തൂന്മാർ.

But nouns in ർ or ഴ് change the final ർ into റി, and ഴ് or ഴ into ഴി, and are declined precisely as വില്ല; as വെർ a root വെറിന്റെ. കീഴ, inferior, below, കീഴിന്റെ. പുകഴ്ച Praise പുകഴ്ചിന്റെ or more commonly പുകഴ്ചി.

It remains to speak of nouns ending in *u*, and in *o*; the first are declined with this slight variation like വില്ല namely, they add വി after the final *u* in the oblique case, except in the vocative in which വെ is added as വസ്തു a thing, വസ്തുവിന്റെ. വസ്തുവിന, വസ്തുവിനെ, voc. വസ്തുവെ, abl. വസ്തുവിൽ, വസ്തുവിനൊട, വസ്തുവിനാൽ, വസ്തുവിൽനിന്ന; In the same manner ബന്ധു a friend, ബന്ധുവിന്റെ, ശത്രു an Enemy, ശത്രുവിന്റെ, ജന്തു a beast, ജന്തുവിന്റെ, പ്രഭു a Prince, പ്രഭുവിന്റെ, ഹെതു a cause, ഹെതുവിന്റെ, these are also declined in the plural like വില്ലുകൾ, only that they double ക into ക്ക thus പ്രഭുക്കൾ Princes, പ്രഭുക്കളുടെ; വസ്തുക്കൾ things, വസ്തുക്കളുടെ.

Nouns which end in ം *m* are declined in the singular like വില്ല but change the final ം into ത്ത, or rather ത്തി, except in in the vocative, in which the ſign െ is added as in പിള്ള as fol-fows, ആകാശം, heaven, gen. ആകാശത്തിന്റെ, Dat. ആകാശത്തിന, acc. ആകാശത്തിനെ or ആകാശത്തെ, voc. ആകാശമെ abl. ആകാശത്തിൽ, 2d ആകാശത്തിനോട, 3d ആകാശത്താൽ, 4th ആകാശത്തിൽനിന്ന.

It may be remarked that theſe nouns may end in all their caſes in ത്ത thus, gen. ആകാശത്ത, Dat. ആകാശത്ത, acc. ആകാശത്ത, 1ſt abla. ആകാശത്ത, 2d ആകാശത്ത 3d ആകാശത്തോട, 4th ആകാശത്തനിന്ന.

Secondy obſerve that this ſort of nouns as well as ſome others of this declenſion, beſides the termination ഇന്റെ may end in ഇലെ, or ഇനുടെ, or in ഉടെ; Ex. gr. ആകാശം gen. ആകാശത്തിന്റെ, or ആകാശത്തിലെ, or ആകാശത്തിനുടെ, or ആകാശത്തോടെ, the laſt is ſeldom uſed by the Malabars except in poetry; But in conformity with this rule it is a good expreſſion to ſay വീട്ടിലെവസ്തു house affairs, നാട്ടിലെരാജാവ the king of a country.

Thirdly that nouns ending in ം have alſo in the ſingular number another dative, by adding to the ablative in ഇൽ the particle ഏക്ക, as from ആകാശത്തിൽ in heaven, Dat. ആകാശത്തിലേക്ക to heaven; രാജ്യത്തിലേക്ക tc the king-dom; This mode of ſpeech is little uſed in common diſ-courſe; it is better to add the ſyllable ഏക്ക to the indeclinable noun in ത്ത, as ആകാശത്തേക്ക. രാജ്യത്തേക്ക.

Fourthly obſerve that theſe nouns in ം have alſo a different form

form of the ablative, by adding to the indeclinable noun the terminations following ഉങ്കൽ, or ിങ്കൽ; thus ആകാശത്തുങ്കൽ, or ആകാശത്തിങ്കൽ at, or in heaven, ഭൂമിയിങ്കൽ at, or on Earth; to this form of the ablative is sometimes added the particle നിന്നു, as ആകാശത്തിങ്കൽനിന്നു from heaven, രാജ്യത്തിങ്കൽനിന്നു from the kingdom. Sometimes indeed the ablative is formed by adding only ൽ to the indeclinable noun, thus ആകാശത്തിൽ in heaven, കുപ്പായത്തിൽ in a coat, മരത്തിൽ in a tree. This mode may also be applied to nouns ending in *a* short, and even to some few others; thus കഴുത്ത the neck, may make കഴുത്തിൽ, as കാൽ the foot, കാൽക്കൽ, or more usually കാക്കൽ വാതിൽ, a door വാതിക്കൽ.

Nouns of the second declension also in ി often follow this rule, as പള്ളി a church പള്ളിക്കൽ: മുറി a bed chamber മുറിക്കൽ.

But we proceed to speak of nouns of the 2d declension: these end, as before observed, in അ or in ി; the first generally drops the *a* or changes it into *e*, adding െട for the genitive, and ക്ക for the Dative. E. g. തല, a Hill, gen. തലെട, dat. തലക്ക, acc. തലെ, or തലെയെ, voc. തലെ, abl. തലയിൽ, 2d തലയാട, 3d തലയാൽ, 4th തലയിൽനിന്നു; so also പട war, gen. പടെട. കഥ a story കഥെട; they may also end in ുടെ, so that it is indifferently said തലെട or തലയുടെ of the head; and പടയുടെ of war.

But

But the words ഉമ്മാ a matron, or lady (applied to musſulman women) അമ്മാ a mother (applied to Hindu women) and some others like these, or compounded of them, make in the genitive യുടെ; thus ഉമ്മാടെ, or ഉമ്മയുടെ; അമ്മയുടെ or അമ്മാടെ.

These nouns are declined in the plural like വിളക്കുകൾ; the long *a* of the singular is not written, or expreſsed, but lightly accented; thus it is written മലകൾ mountains, മലകളുടെ. പടകൾ. പടകളുടെ, where the ദീൎഘം or sign ാ, which gives the power of *a* long, is dropped.

Exceptions to this rule are ഉമ്മാ, & അമ്മാ, and some other nouns signifying rational beings which take മാർ in the plural, like those of the first declension which have been noticed; thus ഉമ്മമാർ and അമ്മമാർ

Nouns in ം it should have been observed, instead of കൾ, in the plural, have ങ്ങൾ, and are declined like വിളക്കുകൾ, altering the termination to ങ്ങൾ.

It remains only to treat of nouns ending in ി or ീ; theſe add ിടെ in the genitive; without the additional *i*, in this manner യുടെ, but in the, dative they add to the final ി the particle ക്ക, thus സ്ത്രീ a woman, genitive. സ്ത്രീയുടെ, dat സ്ത്രീക്ക, acc. സ്ത്രീടെ, or സ്ത്രീയെയെ, voc. സ്ത്രീയെ. abl. സ്ത്രീയിൽ, &c. പള്ളി the church; genitive. പള്ളിയുടെ; dat. പള്ളിക്ക. തീ fire, abl. തീയിൽ &c.

There are however different forms of the genitive by adding

ding, to the termination ി, only ടെ, as സ്ത്രീടെ of a woman, പത്നിടെ, or യുടെ, as സ്ത്രീയുടെ, പത്നിയുടെ, and from പുലി a tyger, is formed with equal propriety പുലിയുടെ. പുലിടെ, or പുലിയടെ.

These nouns are declined in the plural like വിള്ളികൾ, by adding to the final ി of the singular കൾ or കൾ. But if they be the names of rational creatures they may be declined with the particle മാർ, like ഉമ്മമാർ; thus സഖി a friend makes സഖികൾ and സഖിമാർ; and ചെട്ടി a merchant, or trader ചെട്ടികൾ or ചെട്ടിമാർ.

But remember the particle മാർ is very rarely used, and indeed only in some sanscrit words. It is always better to say കൾ, thus പടയാളി a soldier, makes പടയാളികൾ, and not പടയാളിമാർ.

LECTURE SECOND,

Of the Gender, and formation of the nouns, and of the adjective.

SECTION 1st.

Of certain adjectives which require to be placed after the substantive.

As this sort of adjectives stand singly exceptions to a general rule, let us begin with them. They correspond with our expressions all, every, and are as follow; ഒക്ക or ഒക്കയും, and എല്ലാരും or എല്ലാവരും which serve for both masculine and

and feminine genders, and എല്ലാം for the neuter. They are declined in form following; nom. ഒക്ക gen. ഒക്കയുടെ, or ഒക്കയുടെയും, dat. ഒക്കക്ക, or ഒക്കക്കും, acc. and voc. ഒക്ക, or ഒക്കയും abl. ഒക്കയിൽ or ഒക്കയിലും, 2d ഒക്കയൊട or ഒക്കയൊടും, 3d ഒക്കയാൽ or ഒക്കയാലും, 4th ഒക്കയിൽനിന്ന.

Observe that nouns placed before this word may be declined, or not; Ex. gr. മാനുഷർഒക്കയുടെയും of all men, ക്രിസ്ത്യാനികൾഒക്കക്കും to all Christians, സ്ത്രീകളിൽഒക്കയിലും in all women. Nom. എല്ലാരും, or എല്ലാവരും, or എല്ലാവരെയും, all. Gen. എല്ലാരുടെയും, or എല്ലാവരുടെയും of all. Dat. എല്ലാർക്കും, or എല്ലാവർക്കും to all. Acc. and Voc. like the nom. Abl. എല്ലാരിലും, or എല്ലാവരിലും in all 2d എല്ലാരൊടും, or എല്ലാവരൊടും, 3d എല്ലാരാലും, or എല്ലാവരാലും, 4th എല്ലാരിലുംനിന്ന, or എല്ലാവരിലുംനിന്ന from all.

The latter of these expressions is the best.

These words serve only for the masculine and feminine genders മാനുഷർഎല്ലാരും, or എല്ലാവരെയും all men, ശാസ്ത്രികൾഎല്ലാവർക്കും to all learned, സ്ത്രീകൾഎല്ലാവരുടെയും of all women.

Nouns placed before this adjective may be sometimes tho' seldom declined, and not in all cases, as intimated before.

In the same manner the two following words are placed after nouns substantive in the nominative only, or perhaps in in any other viz. case എല്ലാരും, and എല്ലാരെല്ലാരും all, മനുഷ്യരെല്ലാരും all mankind.

But with neuter nouns the Malabarians use the following word എല്ലാം, which is thus declined, nom. എല്ലാം all. Gen. എല്ലാറ്റിന്റെ, or എല്ലാറ്റിന്റെയും, Dat. എല്ലാറ്റിന്നു, or എല്ലാറ്റിനും; accus. എല്ലാം, or എല്ലാറ്റെ, or എല്ലാറ്റിനെ, or എല്ലാറ്റിനെയും; abl. എല്ലാറ്റിൽ, or എല്ലാറ്റിലും, എല്ലായിൽ, or എല്ലായിലും in all, 2d എല്ലാറ്റോട, or എല്ലാറ്റിനോടും with all, 3d എല്ലാറ്റാൽ or എല്ലാറ്റിനാൽ by, or through all, 4th എല്ലാറ്റിൽ, or എല്ലാറ്റിലുംനിന്നു from all; നെല്ലെല്ലാം all the rice, പട്ടാളമെല്ലാം all the army, മൃഗങ്ങളെല്ലാം all the animals, ഇതെല്ലാം all this.

SECTION 2d.

Of the Gender, and formation of the noun.

In the Malabar Language the names of God, angels, Demons, and men; are of the masculine Gender; so തമ്പുരാൻ, or ദൈവം God; മനുഷ്യൻ man; ദൈത്യൻ, or പിശാച a Demon, മാലാഖ, or ദെവദൂതൻ (the samscrit term) an angel.

Nouns relating to the female sex are feminine, as സ്ത്രീ a woman; കന്യാസ്ത്രീ a virgin; പെണ്ണാൾ a woman, and പെണ്ണു a female.

All other nouns whether the names of animals, or senseless things, are neuter; as ആകാശം heaven, സമുദ്രം the sea, മൃഗം an an animal, കുരങ്ങ a monkey, തത്ത a Parrot; all theſe, according to their terminations, are reduced to two declenſions already explained.

SECTION 3d.

Of adjectives, and their formation.

Adjectives in this language are indeclinable, and, with a few exceptions, are always placed before their ſubſtantives. Thus നല്ല good, വെളുത്ത white, കറുത്ത black, join with nouns ſubſtantive in this manner, നല്ലമാനുഷൻ a good man, നല്ലസ്ത്രീ a good woman, നല്ലമൃഗം a good animal.

Adjectives may be formed from nouns ſubſtantive by means of the participle of the verb ആകുന്നു I am, being placed between two nouns. This radical participle is ഉള്ള; the ſame is done with ആകുന്ന, and ആയ; thus from the nouns മാന honor, and സ്ത്രീ a woman, comes മാനമുള്ളസ്ത്രീ an honorable woman, from പാപം a ſin, and പ്രവൃത്തി a work, പാപം ആകുന്നപ്രവൃത്തി a ſinful action, മഹത്വം ആയമന്ത്രം a glorious myſtery, വിലയം ആയവസ്തു a precious thing.

But if you place between two nouns the radical participle of the negative verb ഇല്ല, which is ഇല്ലാത്ത, you will have a negative adjective, thus, മാനമില്ലാത്തസ്ത്രീ a woman without honor, അറിവില്ലാത്തആൾ an ignorant perſon, പേടി ഇല്ലാത്തമാനുഷൻ a dauntleſs man.

Obſerve firſt that adjectives become, or have the power of ſubſtantives

substantives when the pronoun അവൻ, അവൾ, അത he, she, it, is joined to the radical participle, but the initial അ is dropped, or rather absorbed in the preceding letter, and only വൻ. വൾ. ത is pronounced. Thus നല്ലമനുഷ്യൻ, and നല്ലവൻ indifferently signify a good man, and നല്ലസ്ത്രീ and നല്ലവൾ have the same sense, so also have കീൎത്തിയുള്ളസ്ത്രീ, and കീൎത്തിയുള്ളവൾ. പെരിടുള്ളൊരകമനുഷ്യൻ and, പെരിടുള്ളൊരകവൻ, and they are declined like the pronouns in which they terminate.

Secondly, adjectives are formed from the radical participles of any verbs whatever, as ചത്തപശു a dead cow, ഉണങ്ങിയനെല്ല dried rice, കഴിഞ്ഞവെനിൽ the past summer.

Thirdly, they are formed by adding to substantives the particle പെട്ട, which is the radical participle of the verb പെടുന്നു, thus from കീൎത്തി fame, comes കീൎത്തിപ്പെട്ടവൻ, കീൎത്തിപെട്ടവൾ, or കീൎത്തിപെട്ടമനുഷ്യൻ, കീൎത്തിപെട്ടസ്ത്രീ, an honorable, or celebrated man, or woman, and കീൎത്തിപെട്ട നഗരി a famed city, ബഹുമാനപ്പെട്ടയാൾ an illustrious person. But this form of speech is not universal. Sometimes also in place of പ്പെട്ട they write ആകപ്പെട്ട; thus, from നരക. Hell, comes നരകംആകപ്പെട്ടവൻ one devoted to Hell, from ശരണം hope, is made ശരണംആകപ്പെട്ടവൻ hoping, full of hope.

Fourthly, adjectives are made from nouns ending in ം, by leaving out this final letter, and adding another substantive, in in this manner, of മാൎഗ്ഗം, law, is formed മാൎഗ്ഗമൎയ്യാദ legal custom, മരണം Death മരണപ്രമാദം the danger of death, മരണസമയം the approach of death. Sometimes, but not often, adjectives are similarly made of other nouns not ending in ം. പള്ളിക്കാൎയ്യം Church affairs, പള്ളിത്താക്കോൽ the Church key.

But if this sort of adjectives be formed from nouns in ട or റ, the first is changed into ട്ട, and റ into റ്റ; as, from വീട a house വീട്ടുകാൎയ്യം house affairs. But this mode should be rarely used.

Let it be well remembered that some nouns also, nay even adverbs, are made adjectives in this way by adding to them the particle ത്തെ, as, മാൎഗ്ഗം, the Law, becomes മാൎഗ്ഗത്തെ മൎയ്യാദ lawful custom; കഴിഞ്ഞാണ്ട the past year, കഴിഞ്ഞാണ്ടത്തെപെരുനാൾ last years festival; ഇപ്പോൾ now, is made ഇപ്പോഴത്തെസങ്കടം present greivance; ഇന്നലെ yesterday ഇന്നലത്തെകാൎയ്യം yesterday's business.

All neuter nouns become adjectives by adding to them the termination കാരൻ, and nouns of the feminine gender by adding കാരത്തി, thus ബുദ്ധി signifies prudence, ബുദ്ധികാരൻ a prudent man, ബുദ്ധികാരത്തി, a prudent woman, ഇതാലിയ Italy, ഇതാലിയക്കാരൻ an Italian, കൊച്ചി Cochin, കൊച്ചിക്കാരൻ a Cochinese.

But if the nouns end in ം this must be dropped, and കാരൻ, or കാരത്തി is added to the preceding letter, thus

മൊ

ഭാഗ്യം happiness, makes ഭാഗ്യക്കാരൻ and ഭാഗ്യക്കാരത്തി; but if the noun end in ട, this letter is changed into ട്ടു, thus നാട a country, നാട്ടുകാരൻ, a native, വീട a house, വീട്ടുകാരൻ, and തറവാട്ടുകാരൻ from തറവാട a man of noble birth, or family.

Lastly, it may be remarked that some nouns are made adjectives only by adding ൻ, or, ഇ, or ത്തി instead of കാരൻ, and കാരത്തി; as ശുദ്ധം sanctity, ശുദ്ധൻ, and ശുദ്ധി, or ശുദ്ധത്തി a holy-man, or woman; വയറ the belly, വയറൻ and വയറി a fat-man, or woman; ലുബ്ധൻ, ലുബ്ധത്തി, a miser, or crone. But this will suffice.

SECTION 4th.

Of Numerals, and of Comparatives, and Superlatives.

The numerals are ഒന്ന, രണ്ട, മൂന്ന, one, two, three &c &c. as may be seen at the end of the alphabet, and are placed without variation before all nouns, thus രണ്ടുകാലം two years, മൂന്നാളുകൾ three persons, അഞ്ചുമാസത്തിങ്കൽ in five months; they may therefore be considered as adjectives.

Observe that ഒന്ന, when joined with a noun, is changed to ഒരു, or ഒര, as ഒരജന്തു one animal, ഒരുഗ്രന്ഥം one book, ഒരുസ്ത്രീ one woman.

The cardinal numbers become ordinals by adding the particle ആം, or thus ാം; as ഒന്നാംദിവസം the first day, രണ്ടാംപക്കം the second day, മൂന്നാംപക്കം the third day, അഞ്ചാംവർഗ്ഗം the fifth head, or chapter, നാല്പതാംദി

വസം

ശെഷം the 40th fable, ഇരുവതാംദിവസം the twentieth day.

There is another way of making adjectives of these numerals; which is by adding the particle വൻ, or വൾ contracted from അവൻ, അവൾ, to the ordinal formed as above. Thus ഒന്നാമവൻ the first, രണ്ടാമവൻ the second, മൂന്നാമവൻ the third; but when in reckoning they assume the form of an adverb, we then say ഒന്നാമത firstly, രണ്ടാമത 2dly, മൂന്നാമത thirdly, നാലാമത fourthly.

Observe; that of the word ഒരു are formed other adjectives in the following manner; ഓരൊന്ന each, and ഓരൊരൊ every, of the neuter gender, as ഓരൊരൊപടയാളി every soldier, ഓരൊരൊകഥ every story, ഓരൊരൊകാൎയ്യം every affair. In the plural it makes ഓരൊരൊകഥകൾ, ഓരൊരൊകാൎയ്യങ്ങൾ; from these also are formed ഓരൊരൊരുത്തൻ ഓരൊരൊരുത്തി every one, which are declined like പുരുഷൻ, and സ്ത്രീ.

Also that in counting persons we say ഓരൊരൊരുത്തൻ one by one, ഇരുവര two and two, മൂവര by threes, നാല്വര by fours, അഞ്ചുവര by fives. But speaking of brutes, or inanimate things we say ഓരൊന്ന. ഈരണ്ട. മുമ്മൂന്ന. നന്നാല. അഞ്ചഞ്ച. But in putting money out at interest we express it thus, അഞ്ചിന ഒന്ന one for five, പത്തിന രണ്ട two for ten. നൂററിന പത്ത ten for a hundred, or 10 per cent. But in summing up an account we say പതിററണ്ടിരുവത twice ten

ten is twenty, പതിററമൂന്നുകൂട്ടുക three times ten is thirty, പതിററപത്തനൂറ ten times ten is a hundred.

It is to be especially remembered that these numerical nouns are declined in certain cases, thus ഒന്നു gen. ഒന്നിനെറ. Dat. ഒന്നിന്നു, and രണ്ടിന്നു. മൂന്നിന്നു. നൂറ a hundred, gen. നൂററിനെറ, dat. നൂററിന്നു, abl. നൂററാൽ.

And it may not be much out of its place to remark here, that even adverbs are sometimes declined, or made adjectives as, പണ്ടു formerly, പണ്ടെത്തകാലങ്ങളിൽ in ancient times, ഇപ്പോൾ, now, makes ഇപ്പോഴെത്തവൎത്തമാനം present circumstances, or news.

To proceed to the comparatives and Superlatives. These in the Malabar Language, properly speaking, are wanting; but the defect is supplied two ways. First, when any comparison is to be made, by means of the prepositions കാൾ, or കാളിൽ, or കാട്ടിലും, or കാളിലും, or കാളും, which all signify above. Then the thing, or person with which comparison is made must be put in the accusative case, and the person, or thing compared in the Nominative, thus, the sun is larger than the Earth ഭൂമിയെക്കാട്ടിലും എത്രം വലിയത, sanctity is better than science ശാസ്ത്രത്തെക്കാളിലും പുണ്യം നല്ലു, or sanctity is good above science.

But the more elegant way is to put the thing, or person to which you would compare another in the ablative in ഇൽ, as ഭൂമിയിൽ എത്രംവലിയത, ശാസ്ത്രത്തിൽപുണ്യം ന

ല്ലു

ള്ളു as above; പിഴെക്കാറ്റിലുംമരിക്കനല്ലു death is preferable to ſin.

Sometimes, by way of interrogation, the comparative is uſed in this manner ഏതനല്ലു മീനൊ ഇറച്ചിയൊ which is better (literally, good) fiſh, or fleſh, and so in other inſtances.

The Malabar Idiom is also defective in the superlative degree properly so called, but supplies the want by certain adverbs, which signify very, or much ഏറ്റം, പെരിക, or വളരെ, and sometimes, for greater emphaſis, they double the said adverbs, as നന്ന good, ഏറ്റംനന്ന the best, വലിയക്ലെശം great distreſs, ഏറ്റംവലിയക്ലെശം the greateſt affliction, ബഹുമാനപ്പെട്ട illuſtrious, ഏറ്റംബഹുമാനപ്പെട്ട moſt noble, or illuſtrious. This mode of expreſſion is common in other oriental languages, particularly the Hebrew, as in the Evangeliſt ഏറ്റംവലിയസന്തൊഷകാര്യസന്തൊഷിച്ചു they rejoiced with exceeding great Joy.

LECTURE THIRD,

OF PRONOUNS.

SECTION 1ſt.

Pronouns in this, as in other languages are declined ഞാൻ I, എന്റെ of me, എനിക്ക to me, acc. and voc. എന്ന abl. എന്നാൽ &c. Plural ഞങ്ങൾ we, ഞങ്ങളുടെ of us, ഞങ്ങൾക്ക to us, and ſo on.

Nom.

Nom. നാം I, or we, gen. നമ്മടെ, dat. നമ്മക്ക, acc. ന മ്മെ. In the plural ഞങ്ങൾ is always used. This pronoun of distinction is only used by princes and great men. In religious discourses too it is commonly used as ഞങ്ങളുടെതമ്പുരാൻ our God.

Observe that instead of ഞങ്ങളുടെ, the Malabars frequently say ഞങ്ങടെ of us, as they do നിങ്ങടെ of you; and അവര ടെ, and ഇവരടെ for അവരുടെ, and ഇവരുടെ of him.

SECTION 2d.

Of the pronoun of the second person.

Nom. നീ you, or thou, Gen. നിന്റെ Dat. നിനക്ക Acc. നിന്നെ Voc. നീയെ but when we call a person, if a Male, say, എടാനീ, if a female എടീനീ and sometimes, omitting നീ, we say only എടാ, or എടീ E. G. ഇവിടുന്നുപൊഎടാ, go you from hence, ഇങ്ങുവാഎടീ come you hither. Speaking to a man, or woman; but this is inelegant.

The honorary pronoun of the second, or perhaps third person, is താൻ Gen. തന്റെ Dat. തനിക്ക Voc. rarely used, Acc. തന്നെ: In the plu. it would make തങ്ങൾ Gen. തങ്ങ ളുടെ, but this is not in use in conversation between equals.

With respect to this pronoun it may be remarked that നീ is addressed to persons only of low condition, or to Children; In general speaking to men we say താൻ, and to women unless of the lowest order നിങ്ങൾ; thus you cannot say to a female

നീ

നീയെന്തിന വന്നു why are you come? but, നിങ്ങളെന്തിന വന്നു, നിങ്ങൾ പെടിക്കണ്ട do not be alarmed. Sometimes indeed this form of expreſſion is uſed to men, and it may be a greater mark of diſtinction than താൻ, thus നിങ്ങളെവിടെക്കപൊകുന്നു where is your highneſs going?

Secondly obſerve that the Malabars in ſpeaking to a king, or great perſonage make uſe of a still more reſpectful expreſſion, which may anſwer to your Majesty അങ്ങ, or അങ്ങു, Gen. അങ്ങെവരെ, Dat. അങ്ങെക്ക, Acc. അങ്ങെ, the other caſes are wanting, as അങ്ങുകല്പിച്ചാൽമതി it is enough that your Majesty command me. അങ്ങെക്കാരൊഗ്യക്കെടൊ are you ill? അങ്ങെ, or അങ്ങെവരെകാൎയ്യം your highneſs's affairs.

But in addreſſing a Raja, or his Miniſter, to avoid offence, it is uſual to repeat the name രാജാവ, and കാൎയ്യക്കാരൻ in whatever caſe the ſentence may require.

SECTION 3d.

Of Pronouns of the third perſon.

Theſe are അവൻ. അവൾ. അത. He, ſhe, it, or that, ഇവൻ. ഇവൾ. ഇത. this, maſc. fem. and neuter; ഏവൻ, ഏവൾ, ഏത who, what? They are declined like പുത്രൻ, or നിങ്ങൾ, or like വിള; but this laſt pronoun is not in uſe except in the neuter gender ഏത which, or what.

The plural of theſe pronouns is common to the maſculine, and

and fem. genders, thus അവൻ makes അവർ both for male, or female, and is declined like പുത്രൻ, but the neuter has no plural അത, ഇത, എത.

The honorary pronoun of the third person is അദ്ദേഹം that personage, Gen. അദ്ദേഹത്തിന്റെ, Dat. അദ്ദേഹത്തിന; in the same manner ഇദ്ദേഹം, Dat. ഇദ്ദേഹത്തിന, so in speaking of a great man we must say ഇദ്ദേഹംചെയ്തതനല്ലതാകുന്നു, and not ഇവൻചെയ്തതനല്ലതാകുന്നു, what that person did is good, which last would be used only in regard to inferiors, അദ്ദേഹംപറഞ്ഞതകൊള്ളാം what he said is right.

But when we speak reverentially of the female sex the plural is used for the singular അവർ, ഇവർ, as അവർമരിച്ചു she is dead, ഇവർനിന്റെകെട്ടിയവളൊ is she your wife? to young girls, or people of the lowest rank, only, do we use the singular അവൾ, ഇവൾ.

It must be remembered that these are substantive pronouns so that we can never say അവൻകാര്യക്കാരൻ, ഇവൻപുത്രൻ, അതവസ്തു that thing, ഇപ്പെണ്ണ this woman, ഇക്കാലം this year or this time, but ആകാര്യക്കാരൻ, ഇപ്പുത്രൻ, അവസ്തു, ഇപ്പെണ്ണ, ഇക്കാലം.

SECTION 4th.

Of Possessive Pronouns.

There being no distinct pronouns of this class, in the Malabar language, to express them the genitive cases of the preceding primitives are used in all genders, and numbers as the sentence

sentence may require. E. G. my book എന്റെ പുസ്തകം, my sins എന്റെ ദൊഷങ്ങൾ, your will നിന്റെ മനസ്സ, thy Father നിന്റെ അപ്പൻ, his business അവന്റെ കാര്യം.

According to the distinctions of rank we use the common, or what I have called honorary pronouns. The possessive pronoun is also supplied by placing the participle ഉള്ള between the person, or thing possessing in the dative, and the thing possessed in the nominative, as എനിക്കുള്ള വീട my house, നിനക്കുള്ള വസ്തു the thing belonging to you, പള്ളിക്കുള്ള ദ്രവ്യം the money belonging to the church.

Sometimes indeed this participle is used as it were in the abstract sense, as എനിക്കുള്ളത mine, നിനക്കുള്ളത thine അവക്കുള്ളത His, as എനിക്കുള്ളതും നിനക്കുള്ളതും ഇവിടെ ഇല്ല here is neither yours, or mine.

SECTION 5th.

Of Relatives.

The want of relatives in this language, which is supplied by the participles of verbs, seems to promise, and does really occasion serious difficulties to learners; the manner of expressing them will be best explained by Examples; as, the woman whom thou gavest me as a companion hath beguiled me കൂട്ടായിട്ട എനിക്ക തന്ന സ്ത്രീ എന്നെ ചതിച്ചു, literally, giving, or having given to me a woman, she has deceived me, അന്നെ മെച്ചമായിട്ട പറഞ്ഞ തത്ത പറന്നുപൊയി the parrot, which

which talked so well is flown away, എന്നെപെററഅമ്മ the mother who bore me, പ്രായശ്ചിത്തംചെയ്യുന്നൊരുപാപക്കാരൻ the sinner who performs penance, നമ്മുടെആത്മാവിനെഅശുദ്ധമാക്കുന്നൊരുപാപം The sin which defileth our souls, തമ്പുരാനെആരാധിക്കുന്നൊരുപൈതൽ the Boy who worships God.

This sort of relative is also formed by adding to the participles, as above, the pronoun അവൻ, or അവൾ, as, he who walketh in the paths of virtue shall receive the blessing പുണ്യത്തിന്റെമാർഗ്ഗത്തിൽനടക്കുന്നവൻചെല്ലാത്തക്കിട്ടും; this form is also used for the neuter by adding അത, as അവൻചെയ്തതൊപാപം what he committed was a sin, നീപറഞ്ഞതുകെട്ടില്ല I did not hear what you said.

But when we would use the interrogative, who? in the masculine, or feminine, we say ആര് both in singular, and plural, as ആരവന്നു who is come, ആരപൊയി who went? ഇതുചെയ്തതാര who did this?

Observe that this pronoun is most commonly joined to verbs in the neuter radical participle, as പൊയതാര who is gone? ചത്തതാര who is dead? നിന്നെസൃഷ്ടിച്ചതാര who created you? It is declined thus, Nom. ആര് Gen. ആരുടെ Dat. ആൎക്ക acc. ആരെ abl. ആരാൽ 2d, ആരൊട 3d, ആരിൽ.

The neuter interrogative pronoun what? is expressed by എന്ത്; or എന്ത, or എന്തു as, എന്തവെണ്ടു what do you want? or or ഏതുവെന്നു; ഇതിലേതു which of these? But ഏത, or ഏതു have no other case than the dative as, ഏതിന to what? ഏതിനവന്നു for what are you come? ഇതെന്തിനവന്നു what has this come for, ഇതെന്തിനാകുന്നു to what purpose is this?

The particle self, which is often subjoined to pronouns, as myself, yourself, is expressed by adding തന്നെ, as ഞാൻ തന്നെ I myself, നീതന്നെ thou thyself, or നിങ്ങൾതന്നെ you yourself, അവൻതന്നെ he himself, അതതന്നെ that same.

But it is to be remembered that തന്നെ is very frequently used for the adverb solely, alone, as ഞാൻതന്നെ I only, ഞാൻതന്നെ ഉണ്ടായിരുന്നു I alone was there, ഞാൻതന്നെ ശേഷിച്ചു I was left alone, ഇതതന്നെ ഉള്ളു there is only this, അതതന്നെ അല്ല not only that.

It will be necessary to say somthing of the affirmative, and negative pronouns. Of the first class are ആരാനും some one, which has only the genitive ആരാന്റെ, as also it, compound മറ്റാരാനും any other, മറ്റാരാന്റെ; but the neuter, any thing, is expressed by ഏതാനും, as, is there any news? ഏതാനും വർത്തമാനം, or ഏതാനും വർത്തമാനം ഉണ്ടൊ; മറ്റവൻ another മറ്റവൾ, മറ്റെത, മറ്റൊരുത്തൻ, മറ്റൊരുത്തി, മറ്റൊന്നു, some other: മിക്കവൻ, or മിക്കവാറും the most part, the generality, and മിക്കതു, the neuter gender, corresponding to our adverb, in general, for the most part; പലർ many, genitive പലരുടെ, and പലെത neuter, ചിലർ, neuter ചിലെത some; വല്ലവർ, or വ

ലെ

ഒലെത്തിവൻ whoever, neuter വലെത്തിക whatever. Theſe in the maſc. gender, which ſerves alſo for the fem. are declined like ഹ്രുൻ.

Obſerve that theſe are more properly ſubſtantive pronouns, but they may be made adjectives, thus പലമനുഷ്യർ many men, പലസ്ത്രീകൾ many women, പലകാര്യം whatever buſineſs.

2dly, that we uſe theſe pronouns to form others correſponding to them, namely by adding പ്പൊഴും, or പ്പൊൾ as മിക്കപ്പൊഴും for the moſt part, വല്ലപ്പൊൾ how often ſo-ever.

Among the negative pronouns may be reckoned the following, ആരും no one, which is declined in the manner following. Nom. ആരും, Gen. ആരുടെയും, Dat. ആർക്കും, Acc. ആരെയും, Abl. ആരാലും, 2d, ആരൊടും; It is uſed thus, ആരത് who is there? ആരുമില്ല there is no one, ആരും വന്നില്ല no one is come. In the ſame manner is declined ഒരുത്തനും no body, or none, gen. ഒരുത്തന്റെയും, dat. ഒരുത്തനുക്കും, acc. ഒരുത്തനെയും, abl. ഒരുത്തനാൽ, ഒരുത്തനാൽ, ഒരുത്തനൊട, or ഒരുത്തനൊടും.

There is another negative pronoun of the neuter gender ഒന്നും nothing, as എന്തത് what is it? ഒന്നുമില്ല it is nothing. It is indeclinable; ſo that if you would expreſs to, or for nothing, you would ſay ഒന്നിനും കൊള്ളുക, or ഒന്നിനും കൊള്ളുകയില്ല it is good for nothing. But enough of nouns, we proceed to

Lecture

LECTURE FOURTH,

Of Verbs, and their Conjugation.

All verbs in the Malabar language are impersonal, and, consequently, are similarly conjugated without variation, and, in strictness of speaking, have only three tenses; the present, the preterite, and the future. The others, corresponding with ours, are supplied by annexing certain particles, of which more will be said hereafter.

The conjugation of the substantive verb ഉണ്ടു I am, Present tense ഞാൻ, നീ, അവൻ, or അവൾ, ഞങ്ങൾ, or നാം, നിങ്ങൾ, അവർ, ഉണ്ടു in all persons.

Imperf. ഉണ്ടായിരുന്നു I was. Preterite ഉണ്ടായി 2d, part ഉണ്ടായിട്ടു in, or by being, 3d, pret ഉണ്ടായശേഷം, or ഉണ്ടായതിൽപിന്നെ after that I was 4th, pret. ഉണ്ടാകകൊണ്ടു because I was.

Preter-plu.-perf. is wanting, but supplied by ഉണ്ടായി. Future ഞാൻ ഉണ്ടാം I will be, ഉണ്ടാകുന്നു I am wont to be, ഉണ്ടാകേണം I must be. Imperative ഉണ്ടാ, or ഉണ്ടാക be thou, and, for the sake of distinction, and respect താൻ ഉണ്ടായാലും; അവൻ ഉണ്ടാകട്ടെ let him be, plu. നാം, or ഞങ്ങൾ ഉണ്ടാ let us be, നിങ്ങൾ ഉണ്ടാകുവിൻ be you, അവരുണ്ടാകട്ടെ let them be.

Optative mood is supplied, in the manner hereafter explained, by means of the conjunction എങ്കിൽ, or എന്നുവരികിൽ if; it may therefore be considered as the same with the

Conditional

CONDITIONAL CONJUNCTIVE എങ്കിൽ,

present ആകുന്നെങ്കിൽ if I be,

Imperf. ആയിരുന്നെങ്കിൽ if I was,

conjunctive എങ്കിലും although,

preterite ആയെങ്കിലും although, I have been,

എപ്പോൾ when,

preterite ആയപ്പോൾ when I have been,

Future ആകുമ്പോൾ when I ſhall be,

Infinitive mood, pre s. ആകുന്നെന്നു to be

pret. ആയെന്നു to have been,

Fut. ആകുമെന്നു to be about to be,

ſupine ആകുവാൻ, or ആവാൻ to be,

Gerunds. 1ſt, ആകേണ്ട which ought to be;

2d, ആകേണ്ടു that it may be;

3d, ആകേണ്ടു or ആകേണ്ടും which muſt be,

4th, ആകേണ്ടുന്നത, ആകേണ്ടുവത in the neuter.

participle, pres. ആകുന്ന being; preter. ആയ that has been, having been, Future ആകുവാനിരിക്കുന്ന which will be.

Conjugation of verb active,

സ്നേഹിക്കുന്നു to love.

Indicative mood,

Preſent ഞാൻ, നീ, അവൻ, ഞങ്ങൾ, നിങ്ങൾ, അവർ സ്നേഹിക്കുന്നു I, thou, he &c. loves.

Preter. Imperf. ഞാൻ &c. സ്നേഹിച്ചിരുന്നു I was loving.

Preterite ഞാൻ സ്നേഹിച്ചു I loved,

2d,

2d, സ്നെഹിച്ചിട്ട് by loving,

3d, സ്നെഹിച്ചാറെ when I loved,

4th, സ്നെഹിച്ചിട്ട because I loved,

Preter-plu. perf. സ്നെഹിച്ചിരുന്നു I had loved,

1st, future സ്നെഹിക്കും I will love,

2d, സ്നെഹിക്കുമാറ് I am used to love,

Imperative mood.

Sing. ഞാൻസ്നെഹിക്ക let me love, നീസ്നെഹി love thou, or more respectfully താൻസ്നെഹിക്കുക, സ്നെഹിക്ക, or still more reverentially താൻസ്നെഹിച്ചാലും; അവൻ, or അയാൻസ്നെഹിക്കട്ടെ let him love.

Plural നാം, or ഞങ്ങൾസ്നെഹിക്കാം, or സ്നെഹിക്കുക let us love, നിങ്ങൾസ്നെഹിപ്പിൻ, love you, അവർസ്നെഹിക്കട്ടെ.

The optative and conjunctive moods are formed by adding to the different tenses of the indicative the particles, if, when, altho' എങ്കിൽ, അപ്പൊൾ, എങ്കിലും E. G. സ്നെഹിക്കുന്നെങ്കിൽ if I love, സ്നെഹിച്ചപ്പൊൾ when I loved, സ്നെഹിക്കുമ്പൊൾ when I shall love, സ്നെഹിച്ചെങ്കിലും altho' I had loved.

Infinitive mood.

Pres. സ്നെഹിക്കുന്നതിന്ന്, to love,

Preterite, സ്നെഹിച്ചതിന്ന് to have loved,

Future സ്നെഹിക്കുമതിന്ന്, to be about to love,

Supine സ്നെഹിക്കാൻ, or more properly സ്നെഹിപ്പാൻ to love.

Part.

Part. സ്നെഹിക്കുന്ന, loving,

Pret. part. സ്നെഹിച്ചു having loved,

Fut. Part സ്നെഹിപ്പാറായിരിക്കുന്ന, to be about to love.

Obſerve that participles may be declined by adding to them the pronouns അവൻ, അവൾ, അതു, as noticed in ſpeaking on the adjective.

LECTURE FIFTH,

On the Conjugation of verbs.

For the more ready formation of verbs it will be uſeful to prefix a few remarks. 1ſt, that all verbs, whether neuter, or active, are conjugated in the ſame manner as the two preceding ഉണ്ടാകുന്നു, and സ്നെഹിക്കുന്നു; 2dly, that all perfect verbs terminate in the pres. indicative in ഉന്നു, as വരുന്നു to come പൊകുന്നു to go; 3dly, that the Malabar Language has no preter: Imperfect which is therefore ſupplied by adding the preterite ഇരുന്നു, of the verb ഇരിക്കുന്നു, to the preterite of the verb to be employed, as, when I came to Rome the holy pontiff Clement the 14th governed the Church of God, ഞാൻ റൊമായിലെക്കു ചെന്നപ്പൊൾ ക്ലെമെന്തു പതിനാലാമനാകുന്ന ശുദ്ധമാന പാപ്പാ തമ്പുരാന്റെ തിരുസ്സഭയെ വാണിരുന്നു. when you came to Verapoli I was at Cochin വന്നപ്പൊൾ ഞാൻ കൊച്ചിയിൽ ഇരുന്നിരുന്നു.

Obſerve here that when the preterite ends in ഉ this is changed into ന which becomes ി, being abſorbed in the initial

initial of the follwing word ഇന്നു, hence you would not write സ്നേഹിച്ചു ഇന്നു I was loving, but സ്നേഹിച്ചിന്നു. But if the preterite ends in യി it is left unchanged and coalesces with the following ഇ thus, it is not written ആയി ഇന്നു I was, but, ആയിന്നു, and കണ്ടിന്നു and not കണ്ടു ഇന്നു I did see.

But sometimes the Malabars use the preterite for the Imperfect, as, when I was going to Cochin I saw him on the road ഞാൻ കൊച്ചിക്കു പോയപ്പോൾ വഴിക്കൽ അവനെ കണ്ടു, when you came I was not at home, നീ വന്നപ്പോൾ ഞാൻ വീട്ടിൽ ഇല്ലാഞ്ഞു; 4th. That all Malabar verbs, except the defectives, or anomalous, end in the preterite in ഉ, or in ഇ, but since they vary even in the preterite, according to the different terminations, I shall lay down certain rules, by which the verb may be easily distinguished, and conjugated.

RULE FIRST.

For determining the Preterite.

All verbs ending in കുന്നു, or ങ്ങുന്നു as also their efficients, or causal verbs, which are made by doubling കുന്നു into ക്കുന്നു make the preter. in യി, leaving out the termination of the present കുന്നു, or ക്കുന്നു, or ങ്ങുന്നു thus.

ആകുന്നു, I am, pret. ആയി.

ഉണ്ടാകുന്നു to have ഉണ്ടായി.

വല്യതാകുന്നു to grow വല്യതായി.

നന്നാകുന്നു to be good, നന്നായി.
കൊള്ളാകുന്നു to be good, കൊള്ളായി.
ചെറുതാകുന്നു to diminish ചെറുതായി.
മതിയാകുന്നു to suffice മതിയായി.
പോകുന്നു to go, പോയി.

In the same manner are formed all verbs compounded of, or derived from, the substantive verb. Their efficients or causals are

ആക്കുന്നു to make, or do ആക്കി,
ഉണ്ടാക്കുന്നു same ഉണ്ടാക്കി,
വലുതാക്കുന്നു to dilate, to enlarge വലുതാക്കി,
പൊക്കുന്നു to raise up, പൊക്കി.

In the same manner are conjugated other verbs in കുന്നു; such as

ഉതകുന്നു to assist ഉതകി,
ഉരുകുന്നു to melt ഉരുകി,
ഉഴുകുന്നു to flow ഉഴുകി,
പഴകുന്നു to be accustomed പഴകി,
ഇറുകുന്നു to be bound ഇറുകി,
കൂകുന്നു or കൂവുന്നു to crow as a cock, കൂകി, or കൂവി;
മുഴുകുന്നു to swim, or dive under water മുഴുകി;
പുൽകുന്നു to embrace പുൽകി,
കഴുകുന്നു to wash plates കഴുകി,
നൽകുന്നു to give നൽകി, (used only in poetry,)
മെഴുകുന്നു to spread a floor with cow dung, മെഴുകി.

The

The compounds of these, or their efficients, perhaps more appropriately causals, have the same preterite, as,

ഉരുക്കുന്നു to cause to melt, or dissolve ഉരുക്കി,
or ഒഴുക്കുന്നു to cause to flow ഒഴുക്കി,
പഴക്കുന്നു to habituate പഴക്കി,
ഇറുക്കുന്നു harden, or to squeeze ഇറുക്കി,

The following are Exceptions from the general rule,
ചാകുന്നു to die, (speaking of brutes) ചത്തു;
പുക്കുന്നു to enter പുക്ക.

The same Preterite have verbs in ങ്ങുന്നു, and their efficients in ക്കുന്നു;

മുങ്ങുന്നു to sink, മുങ്ങി,
മുക്കുന്നു to drown മുക്കി,
പഴുങ്ങുന്നു to grow ripe പഴുങ്ങി,
പഴുക്കുന്നു to make ripe പഴുക്കി,
നീങ്ങുന്നു to recede നീങ്ങി;
നീക്കുന്നു to remove നീക്കി;
അടങ്ങുന്നു to be enclosed അടങ്ങി,
അടക്കുന്നു to include അടക്കി,
കലങ്ങുന്നു to be muddy കലങ്ങി,
കലക്കുന്നു to trouble water കലക്കി,
വെങ്ങുന്നു to grow hot വെങ്ങി,
വെക്കുന്നു to warm വെക്കി, properly വെച്ചു.

Verbs which end in ള്ളുന്നു have also the preterite ending in ണ്ടു, as,

കൊള്ളുന്നു

കൂട്ടുന്നു to call together കൂട്ടി;
വീട്ടുന്നു to discharge (as a debt) വീട്ടി;
ഓട്ടുന്നു to expel ഓട്ടി;
പൂട്ടുന്നു to shut പൂട്ടി;
തട്ടുന്നു to smite, or hammer തട്ടി.

Verbs ending in തു, or ത്തുന്നു form their preterite in the same manner.

കുത്തുന്നു to pierce, or stab കുത്തി;
കൊത്തുന്നു to strike കൊത്തി,
കത്തുന്നു to burn കത്തി,
തത്തുന്നു, to dance തത്തി;
നടത്തുന്നു to make to go നടത്തി,
എത്തുന്നു to arrive, to follow എത്തി,
ഊതുന്നു, to blow ഊതി,
ഉന്തുന്നു, to push back ഉന്തി,
ഓതുന്നു to say prayers ഓതി,
മാന്തുന്നു to scratch മാന്തി.

The same preterite have verbs in ണ്ണ or ണ്ണുന്നു and ള്ളുന്നു, ഴുന്നു and [illegible]ുന്നു as the following.

എണ്ണുന്നു to count എണ്ണി,
നണ്ണുന്നു to be grateful നണ്ണി,
തുള്ളുന്നു to tremble തുള്ളി,
നുള്ളുന്നു to pluck or crop നുള്ളി,
Except ഉണ്ണുന്നു to eat rice ഉണ്ടു,
കൊള്ളുന്നു to buy കൊണ്ടു;

കാണുന്നു to see കണ്ടു,

and വിള്ളുന്നു to split, or cleave വിണ്ടു,

Verbs in റ്റുന്നു, and പ്പുന്നു are as under.

പറ്റുന്നു to stick, പറ്റി;

പഴറ്റുന്നു to disarm പഴറ്റി,

തെറ്റുന്നു to slip തെറ്റി

ഊറ്റുന്നു to fan rice, ഊറ്റി

തുപ്പുന്നു to spit തുപ്പി,

കൂപ്പുന്നു to join the hands in sign of reverence, കൂപ്പി.

Verbs in ന്നുന്നു, and വ്വുന്നു follow this Rule.

മിന്നുന്നു, to shine, മിന്നി,

തെവ്വുന്നു to water തെവി,

തുന്നുന്നു to sew തുന്നി,

മെവ്വുന്നു to equal, or level, obsolete മെവി,

ചിന്നുന്നു to scatter ചിന്നി,

ഊന്നുന്നു to rest on a staff ഊന്നി.

The following are Exceptions.

തിന്നുന്നു to eat തിന്നു,

നൊവ്വുന്നു to feel pain നൊന്തു,

വെവ്വുന്നു or വെകുന്നു to cook, or dress, or burn വെന്തു.

This rule also comprehends verbs ending in ടുന്നു, ണുന്നു, റുന്നു, and ക്കുന്നു when these syllables are preceded by a long vowel as.

ആടുന്നു to dance ആടി,

ചാടുന്നു to leap ചാടി,

ഓടുന്നു

ഓടുന്നു to run ഓടി,

നേടുന്നു to gain നേടി,

വാരുന്നു to collect വാരി,

ഈരുന്നു to ſaw ഈരി,

മൂളുന്നു to mumble മൂളി,

മൂടുന്നു to cover മൂടി,

പാടുന്നു to ſing പാടി,

ഊരുന്നു to unſheath ഊരി,

കോരുന്നു to draw water കോരി,

കാളുന്നു to burn as it were internally. കാളി,

ആളുന്നു to agitate, daſh ആളി,

പാളുന്നു to blaze പാളി.

The following are Exceptions,

തീരുന്നു to finiſh തീർന്നു,

ചേരുന്നു to unite ചേർന്നു,

മീളുന്നു to redeem മീണ്ടു,

നീളുന്നു to be extended നീണ്ടു,

Finally, all verbs follow this rule whiɔh have any two conſonants, other than ന്ന, or ർ before ന്നു, as

മിഞ്ചുന്നു to be ſuper fluous മിഞ്ചി,

മണ്ടുന്നു to run മണ്ടി;

ചിന്തുന്നു, to be poured out ചിന്തി,

മിണ്ടുന്നു to open the mouth മിണ്ടി,

RULE

RULE SECOND.

Verbs active,

And efficient in യിക്കുന്നു, as also the efficients of verbs which end in യുന്നു, and ഴുന്നു, if the termination ക്കുന്നു be preceded by any short vowel, except ഉ, make the preterite in ച്ചു. In the same manner are conjugated all verbs which have any short vocal letter before ക്കുന്നു, unless such as were excepted in the 1st Rule.

കടിക്കുന്നു to bite കടിച്ചു,
പറിക്കുന്നു to rob പറിച്ചു,
ചിരിക്കുന്നു to laugh ചിരിച്ചു,
ചതിക്കുന്നു to deceive ചതിച്ചു.

Except the following

വിക്കുന്നു to smother വിക്കി,
ചിക്കുന്നു to dry rice ചിക്കി.

Effectives of verbs in യുന്നു, and ഴുന്നു, as

ചതെക്കുന്നു to pound ചതെച്ചു from ചതയുന്നു,
ഉറെക്കുന്നു to strengthen ഉറെച്ചു,
ചവെക്കുന്നു to shew ചവെച്ചു,
അയെക്കുന്നു to send അയെച്ചു,
വെക്കുന്നു to put വെച്ചു,
തുണെക്കുന്നു to assist തുണെച്ചു,
പിഴെക്കുന്നു to sin പിഴെച്ചു,

Effectives in യിക്കുന്നു are as follow

കഴിക്കുന്നു to make to pass കഴിച്ചു, from കഴിയുന്നു to pass,

ഇടിക്കുന്നു to derstoy ഇടിച്ചു from ഇടിയുന്നു to be in ruins; വാഴിക്കുന്നു to cause to reign വാഴിച്ചു from വാഴുന്നു to reign വീഴിക്കുന്നു to make to fall വീഴിച്ചു from വീഴുന്നു to fall, തറെക്കുന്നു to drive a nail തറെച്ചു,

EXCEPTIONS.

തുറക്കുന്നു to open തുറന്നു,

അളക്കുന്നു to measure അളന്നു,

അലക്കുന്നു to wash അലക്കി,

ചുമക്കുന്നു to carry on the shoulders ചുമന്നു,

ഇരക്കുന്നു to beg ഇരന്നു,

RULE THIRD.

Verbs neuter, in which ക്കുന്നു is preceded by any short vowel, or vocal consonant, have the preterite in ന്നു as.

ഇരിക്കുന്നു to sit, or be ഇരുന്നു,

കിടക്കുന്നു to lie down കിടന്നു,

പിറക്കുന്നു to be born പിറന്നു,

പറക്കുന്നു to fly പറന്നു,

കടക്കുന്നു to transgress, pass over കടന്നു,

അമക്കുന്നു to be pacified അമന്നു,

വിശക്കുന്നു to hunger വിശന്നു,

നടക്കുന്നു to go, or walk നടന്നു,

പൊളക്കുന്നു to open the month പൊളന്നു,

Except the verb വിറെക്കുന്നു to tremble വിറെച്ചു.

RULE FOURTH.

Verbs which end in ഉക്കുന്നു make the preterite in ഉത്തു as

കൊടു

കൊടുക്കുന്നു to give കൊടുത്തു,
എടുക്കുന്നു to take എടുത്തു,
പകുക്കുന്നു to divide പകുത്തു,
പഴുക്കുന്നു to ripen, പഴുത്തു,
പൊറുക്കുന്നു to suffer പൊറുത്തു,
തടുക്കുന്നു to detain a man തടുത്തു,
അടുക്കുന്നു to approach അടുത്തു.

In the same manner are conjugated verbs in റുക്കുന്നു, as
അറുക്കുന്നു to cut അറുത്തു,

Except.

മുറുക്കുന്നു to bind മുറുക്കി.

RULE FIFTH.

Examples of verbs in രുന്നു,
പകരുന്നു to pour പകൎന്നു,
തുവരുന്നു to be cleaned തുവൎന്നു,
ചുവരുന്നു to drop ചുവൎന്നു,
വളരുന്നു to increase വളൎന്നു,
തകരുന്നു to be broken തകൎന്നു,.

Except the following.

തരുന്നു to give തന്നു,
വരുന്നു to come വന്നു,
പോരുന്നു to come പോന്നു,
പൊരുരുന്നു to contend പൊരുതു.

RULE SIXTH.

Verbs in ച്ചുന്നു have in the Pret. ച്ചു.

അണയുന്നു to approach അണഞ്ഞു,
പറയുന്നു to speak പറഞ്ഞു,
കരയുന്നു to weep കരഞ്ഞു,
അരയുന്നു to rub അരഞ്ഞു,
കഴിയുന്നു to die കഴിഞ്ഞു,
കരിയുന്നു to grow black കരിഞ്ഞു,

But if they double യ into യ്യ the preterite ends in യ്തു, യിതു, or എയിതു as.

എയ്യുന്നു to shoot arrows എയിതു, or എയ്തു,
പെയ്യുന്നു to rain പെയ്തു, or പെയിതു,
നെയ്യുന്നു to weave നെയ്തു, or നെയിതു,
ചെയ്യുന്നു to do, or make ചെയ്തു, or ചെയിതു,
കൊയ്യുന്നു to reap കൊയിതു, or കൊയ്തു.

RULE SEVENTH.

Verbs in ടുന്നു and റുന്നു make ട്ടു, and റ്റു, so that they be not preceded by a long vowel for in that case they make ടി, and റി, as in rule first.

ചുടുന്നു to toast ചുട്ടു,
അകപ്പെടുന്നു to bear അകപ്പെട്ടു,
പെടുന്നു or പടുന്നു to bear പെട്ടു,
ശരണപ്പെടുന്നു to hope, ശരണപ്പെട്ടു,
പാർത്തപ്പെടുന്നു, idem, പാർത്തപ്പെട്ടു,
പ്രിയപ്പെടുന്നു to love പ്രിയപ്പെട്ടു,

RULE

RULE EIGHTH.

Verbs which before ക്കുന്നു take ൾ make the preterite in ട്ടു, but those which, instead of ൾ, have ല make റ്റു

കേൾക്കുന്നു to hear കേട്ടു,

കൾക്കുന്നു, or കക്കുന്നു to rob കട്ടു,

നോല്ക്കുന്നു to fast നോറ്റു,

ഏല്ക്കുന്നു to receive ഏറ്റു,

കൊല്ക്കുന്നു to be beaten കൊറ്റു,

വില്ക്കുന്നു to sell വിറ്റു

Except

നില്ക്കുന്നു to stand നിന്നു,

RULE NINETH.

Verbs in ഴുന്നു make the pret. in ണു and those in ലുന്നു or, ല്ലുന്നു make ന്നു as,

വാഴുന്നു to govern വാണു,

വീഴുന്നു to fall വീണു,

താഴുന്നു to drown താണു,

പുകഴുന്നു to praise പുകഴ്ന്നു,

ഇഴുന്നു to descend ഇണു,

എഴുന്നു to be raised എണു,

കൊല്ലുന്നു to kill കൊന്നു,

അകലുന്നു to be distant അകന്നു,

കാലുന്നു to vomit കാന്നു,

ചെല്ലുന്നു to come to ചെന്നു,

EXCEPT

EXCEPT.

തല്ലുന്നു to ſtrike, തല്ലി,

ചൊല്ലുന്നു to ſpeak ചൊല്ലി, and in poetry alſo ചൊന്നു.

RULE TENTH.

Verbs in ളുന്നു, if the preceding letter be ſhort, or *i*, long, make the preterite in ണ്ടു as

വരളുന്നു to wither വരണ്ടു,

ഉരുളുന്നു to roll ഉരുണ്ടു,

ഇരുളുന്നു to be dark ഇരുണ്ടു,

മീളുന്നു to redeem മീണ്ടു,

കരളുന്നു to gnaw കരണ്ടു,

നീളുന്നു to be ſtretched നീണ്ടു,

പുരളുന്നു to be anointed പുരണ്ടു,

This will be ſufficient for determining preterites.

We proceed to ſay ſomething on the ſecondary preterites, which end in ാൽ, ിട്ടു, ിട്ടാറെ, or കെ. To form the preterite in *al*; where the radical preterite ends in ു, this is changed into ്, adding ആൽ, thus ാ, and ൽ as, സ്നേഹിച്ചാൽ by loving; ചെയ്താൽ by doing; മരിച്ചാൽ by dying; കരഞ്ഞാൽ by weeping; from സ്നേഹിച്ചു, ചെയ്തു, മരിച്ചു, കരഞ്ഞു.

But if the preterite end in ി, this remains, and യാൽ is added as ചൊല്ലിയാൽ by ſpeaking; പൂട്ടിയാൽ by ſhutting, or locking; ഇറങ്ങിയാൽ by deſcending; from ചൊല്ലി, പൂട്ടി, ഇറങ്ങി.

If

If the verbs end in ഞ്ഞു, this is changed into ഞ്ഞ, and ാൽ is added as പറഞ്ഞു makes പറഞ്ഞാൽ. But it is to be remarked that, when this form of ſpeech is uſed, the following verb is to be put in the future tenſe, thus, ദൈവത്തെ സ്നെഹിച്ചാൽ മൊക്ഷം കിട്ടും by loving God you will gain heaven; ഗുണം ചെയ്താൽ ഗുണം കിട്ടും by doing good you will acquire good; തിന്മ ചെയ്താൽ നരകപ്പെടും by doiug ill you will ſuffer damnation.

The preterite in ഞ്ഞിട്ടു is thus formed; if the radical preterite end in ഞ്ഞു nothing more is done but adding ട്ടു as, ഇതു പറഞ്ഞിട്ടു becauſe he ſaid this, from പറഞ്ഞു; but if the preterite end in ഉ, this letter is changed into ഞ്ഞി, and ട്ടു is added, as അതു ചെയ്തിട്ടു പൊയി having done this he departed; അവളെ കണ്ടിട്ടു സ്നെഹിച്ചു I loved after I ſaw her. This form of ſpeech appears from the preceding examples to be rendered ſometimes by, aſter, and becauſe; the firſt of theſe perterites is rendered alſo by the preterite in ഞ്ഞാറെ, which is formed by adding this termination to radicals ending in ഞ്ഞു, as ഇതു പറഞ്ഞാറെ മരിച്ചു having ſaid this, or, after he had ſaid this he died; അവനെ സെവിച്ചാറെ കാൎയ്യം സാധിച്ചു. I obtained my affair after I had paid court to him. This requires to be followed by a preterite.

In the ſouthern diſtrict for ഞ്ഞാറെ they commonly uſe ഞ്ഞാക്കാൽ, as പെണ്ണിനെ കെട്ടിയാക്കാൽ അവളെ ഉപെക്ഷിച്ചു after he had married a wiſe he deſerted her.

Of

Of the preterite plural perfect.

Instead of this tense the preterite is used ,as ഞാനെററംസ്നെഹിച്ചമകനമരിച്ചു the son whom I most loved is dead; മുമ്പ പഠിച്ചകാൎയ്യംമറന്നുപൊയി I have forgotten what I learned before. The Malabars express this tense also by adding ഇരുന്നു to the preterite; as, if I had known this I would have gone with him. ഇതറിഞ്ഞിരുന്നെങ്കിൽകൂടെപൊയിരുന്നു. If he had gone with him to swim he would also have been drowned കൂടെനീന്താൻപൊയെങ്കിൽഅവനുംകൂടെചാകുമായിരുന്നു. It is possible however, from these examples, that ഇരുന്നു may give only the pret. plu. perf. conjunctive.

Of the future.

The future is formed from the present by changing the final ന്നു into ഉം, as സ്നെഹിക്കുന്നു I love, fut. സ്നെഹിക്കും; പൊകുന്നു I go, fut. പൊകും, ചൊല്ലുന്നു I speak ചൊല്ലും; sometimes the future is used for the present but rarely; E. G. വരാപ്പൊഴയിലിരിക്കും അനസ്താസ്യൊസ്പാതിരിക്കുവരുന്നസായൊദം letter coming to the Father Anastasius who lives at Verapoli.

Of the Imperative mood.

The second person of the Imperative is formed by taking away the termination ഉന്നു of the pres nt, and substituing ക, as സ്നെഹിക്കുന്നു I love, Imperative സ്നെഹിക്ക; from ഉറങ്ങുന്നു, ഉറങ്ങ sleep thou; from പൊകുന്നു to go പൊക, or contractedly പൊ.

In

In the ſame way is formed the firſt perſon plural as വിശ്വസിക്ക let us believe, പൊവുക let us go, കളിക്ക let us play.

But in verbs of more than three ſyllables the common imperative is formed by cutting off the final ഉന്നു with its conſonant, as from സ്നെഹിക്കുന്നു imperative സ്നെഹി love thou; ഇരിക്കുന്നു to ſet ഇരി; നടക്കുന്നു to walk നട; കിടക്കുന്നു to lie down, കിട; the ſame happens, in verbs of three ſyllables തരുന്നു to give, താ; വരുന്നു to come, വാ; പൊവുന്നു to go, പൊ, കെൾക്കുന്നു to hear, കെൾ.

In addreſſing great perſonages, another Imperative is uſed which is formed from the preterite in the manner following, namely, if the preterite end in ഉ this is changed into വെണം thus, സ്നെഹിച്ചുവെണം be pleaſed to love; തുറന്നുവെണം open; from സ്നെഹിച്ചു I loved, തുറന്നു I opened; ചിരിച്ചുവെണം ſmile; but when the preterite ends in ഇ, this honorary Imperative is formed by adding thereto ഇവെണം, as ഇറങ്ങിഇവെണം be pleaſed to deſcend, ചൊല്ലിഇവെണം pleaſe to ſpeak.

The ſecond perſon plural of the Imperative mood is formed from the ſupine by changing the termination വാൻ into ഇൻ thus from സ്നെഹിപ്പാൻ to love, സ്നെഹിപ്പിൻ love ye; from ആകുവാൻ to be ആകുവിൻ be you; പൊകുവാൻ is made പൊകുവിൻ go ye.

The third perſon, both ſingular and plural, ſhould rather be called a permiſsive than an imperative mode of ſpeech, and it is formed by changing the ന്നു of the preſent into ആടെ

ട pronounced ſhort, like ഊടെ, as അവൻ, or അവപ്പെണ്ണു സ്നെഹിക്കട്ടെ let him, or her love; വരട്ടെ let him come; ചിരിക്കട്ടെ let him laugh; ഇരിക്കട്ടെ let him ſit. This form includes alſo the firſt as well as third perſons.

Of the Imperative deprecatory affirmative.

The Malabarians uſe this form in their prayers; it is made by changing the penultimate ഉ into െ and adding ണമെ, thus, നമുക്കവെണ്ടിഅപെക്ഷിക്കെണമെ pray for us, from അപെക്ഷിക്കുന്നു; ദൈവമെതമ്പുരാനെഎന്നെരക്ഷിക്കെണമെ ſave me oh my God, from രക്ഷിക്കുന്നു; തരെണമെ give me; സഹായിക്കെണമെ help me. This is uſed only in praying inſtead of the firſt Imperative in അ; it is compounded of the defective verb വെണം it is neceſſary, which is indeed ſometimes uſed in this ſenſe, without undergoing any contraction.

Of the deprecatory negative.

This is formed by changing ഉന്നു into ല്ലെ, or rather അല്ലെ, the firſt ſyllable ſhort, as സ്നെഹിക്കല്ലെ do not love; പൊകല്ലെ do not go, ചെയ്യല്ലെ do not do; ſometimes this is made to end in ല്ലായെ, as പരീക്ഷയിൽ, or പരീക്ഷയിങ്കൽ ഞങ്ങളെ പ്രവെശിപ്പിക്കല്ലായെ lead us not into temptation, or trial.

Of the optative mood.

In the Malabar language there is no regular optative mood; its place is ſupplied by the expreſſion കൊള്ളായിരുന്നു, or നന്നായിരുന്നു it would be well – as, I wiſh the wind would

would blow favorable കാററുള്ളപൊലെ ഊതികിൽ കൊള്ളായിരുന്നു literally, it would be well if the wind blew favorably? would I was dead? ഞാൻ ചത്തു എങ്കിൽ നന്നായിരുന്നു; I wish I had never sinned ഒരുനാളും പിഴച്ചില്ലെങ്കിൽ കൊള്ളായിരുന്നു; I wish we may arrive at Mahe in September കന്നിമാസത്തിങ്കൽ മയ്യഴിക്കു ചെന്നുവെങ്കിൽ കൊള്ളായിരുന്നു.

Of the Conjunctive mood.

This is expressed, in the malabar, by the help of the particles, when, if, although അപ്പൊൾ, എങ്കിൽ, എങ്കിലും added, to the indicative; as, when I was a child I spoke as a child കുഞ്ഞായിരുന്നപ്പൊൾ കുഞ്ഞിനെപ്പൊലെ പറഞ്ഞിരുന്നു; when I was at Rome റൊമായിങ്കൽ ഇരുന്നപ്പൊൾ; when I shall die all will die ഞാൻ ചാകുമ്പൊൾ, or ചാകുംപൊൾ എല്ലാവരും ചാകും; when I shall believe all will believe ഞാൻ വിശ്വസിക്കുംപൊൾ എല്ലാവരെയും വിശ്വസിക്കും; when all shall die I shall remain alone എല്ലാവരും ചത്തിരിക്കുംപൊൾ ഞാൻ ഒന്നു ശെഷിക്കും.

On this head three observations may be made, first that if the particle *when* is joined to the present, or preterite in *u*, the initial അ is cut off, and it is written പ്പൊൾ; but when joined to a preterite in ഇ the അ is changed, and it is written യപ്പൊൾ as ചൊല്ലിയപ്പൊൾ when he spoke, ഉറങ്ങിയപ്പൊൾ when he slept.

2dly. If the particle, when, is joined to the imperfect, the preterite is used instead thereof. As, when I was willing

ള്ള

ഇറങ്ങികൊണ്ടിരുന്നപ്പോൾ, or ഇറങ്ങുകൊണ്ടിരിക്കുമ്പോൾ; when he was going down അവൻ ഇറങ്ങിയപ്പോൾ.

3dly. That when the particle is written, and pronounced പോൾ, as when joined to the future, the final ം/ is left out, and it is written മ്പോൾ as, when I shall love സ്നേഹിക്കുമ്പോൾ.

Of the Conditional എങ്കിൽ, എങ്കിലും.

These conjunctions are added to the present, and preterite as; if I do, or did; ഞാൻ ചെയ്യുന്നു എങ്കിൽ; if you spoke നീ പറഞ്ഞു എങ്കിൽ; altho I love ഞാൻ സ്നേഹിക്കുന്നു എങ്കിലും; If I did this may God punish me ഇത ഞാൻ ചെയ്തു എങ്കിൽ എന്നെ തമ്പുരാൻ ശിക്ഷിക്കട്ടെ; If I said so punish me ഞാൻ പറഞ്ഞു എങ്കിൽ എന്നെ ശിക്ഷിച്ചാലും; although I have sinned I hope to be saved പിഴച്ചു എങ്കിലും രക്ഷപ്പെടുവാൻ ശരണം കാത്തിരിക്കുന്നു.

If he should come it does not signify അവൻ വന്നു എങ്കിൽ വേണ്ടില്ല; Here it is observable that എങ്കിലും is added to verbs without making any change in them whatsoever, either in the present, or preterite.

Of the Infinitive mood.

It is formed by joining the particle എ to the verb, as; സ്നേഹിക്കുന്നു എന്ന, or സ്നേഹിക്കുന്നയെന്ന, to love; സ്നേഹിച്ചു എന്ന to have loved; സ്നേഹിക്കുംയെന്ന, or rather സ്നേഹിക്കുമെന്ന to be about to love.

Of the supine

Verbs which in the present end in ക്കുന്നു, and in the preterite in ച്ചു have the supine in പ്പാൻ, which is done by substituting പ്പാൻ for ക്കുന്നു, as, സ്നേഹിപ്പാൻ to love; ചിരിപ്പാൻ to laugh.

The same supine have verbs in ക്കുന്നു which make the preterite in ത്തു, as; കൊടുപ്പാൻ to give; പൊറുപ്പാൻ to ber.a

Also verbs ending in the preterite in ന്നു, as; നടപ്പാൻ to happen from നടന്നു; ഇരിപ്പാൻ to sit, or be, from ഇരുന്നു, നില്പാൻ to stand, from നില്ക്കുന്നു pret. നിന്നു; ചുമപ്പാൻ from ചുമക്കുന്നു to carry, pret. ചുമന്നു; In fine, all verbs which end in the present in ക്കുന്നു, and in the pret. in ഉ but not in ഇ, make the supine generally in പ്പാൻ.

But verbs in ക്കുന്നു whose pret. ends in ി generally make the supine in വാൻ, as ആകുവാൻ to be, from ആകുന്നു; പോകുവാൻ, to go, from പോകുന്നു; ഒഴുകുവാൻ to flow, from ഒഴുകുന്നു.

In the same manner is formed the supine of all the compounds of ആകുന്നു, which, tho' in the present they end in ക്കുന്നു, have the pret. in ി, as; ഉണ്ടാക്കുവാൻ to make; പൊക്കുവാൻ to raise.

Also verbs in രുന്നു, as, തരുവാൻ, to give; വരുവാൻ to come; വളരുവാൻതുടങ്ങി it began to increase; പോരുവാൻപോകരുതു do not proceed to quarrel.

But verbs which end in ക്കുന്നു pret. ത്തു have the supine പ്പാൻ as

കിപ്പ

തീൎപ്പാൻ to finish, from തീൎക്കുന്നു,
പാൎപ്പാൻ to tarry, from പാൎക്കുന്നു,
വിയൎപ്പാൻ to sweat, from വിയൎക്കുന്നു.

Verbs ending in ല്ലുന്നു; ള്ളുന്നു; also in ടുന്നു, and pret. in ന്ന, or ണ്ടു, ന്നു make the supine in വാൻ, as, ചൊല്ലുവാൻ to say, വീണ്ടുവാൻ to redeem, നേടുവാൻ to acquire, വാഴുവാൻ to govern.

Somtimes however the supine ends in ആൻ by changing the penultimate ഉ into ാ, as കൊല്ലാൻ to kill, ചുടാൻ to roast.

Verbs in യ്യുന്നു make വാൻ in the supine, omitting entirely യ്യുന്നു, as, കരെവാൻ from കരെയ്യുന്നു to weep; പറെവാൻ to speak from പറെയ്യുന്നു.

But if in യ്യുന്നു this യ്യ is changed into ൈ, and വാൻ is added, as പൈവാൻ to rain from പെയ്യുന്നു; ചെയ്‌വാൻ to do from ചെയ്യുന്നു.

All other malabar verbs, whatever be the termination of the present, have the supine in ാൻ, by changing the ഉ penultimate into ആ, as, മുങ്ങാൻ from മുങ്ങുന്നു to sink; അടെക്കാൻ from അടെക്കുന്നു to shut, or lock; മൂടാൻ from മൂടുന്നു to close; എണ്ണാൻ from എണ്ണുന്നു to reckon; വെവാൻ from വെവുന്നു to dress victuals.

The following verb ഉണ്ണുന്നു, to eat rice, is an exception to all these rules, it making the supine ഉണ്മാൻ, and കാണുന്നു to see കാണ്മാൻ, or കാമാൻ, as also തിന്നുന്നു to eat തിന്മാൻ.

Of

Of Gerunds.

Gerunds are compounded of the verb to be used in the sentence, and the defective verb വെണം, or വെണ്ടു, as സ്നെഹിക്കെണ്ടു, സ്നെഹിക്കെണ്ടു which ought to be loved, and സ്നെഹിക്കെണ്ടും, സ്നെഹിക്കെണ്ടുന്ന, സ്നെഹിക്കെണ്ടുക, സ്നെഹിക്കെണ്ടുന്നുക, which must be loved.

Of Participles.

The radical participles of the present, preterite, and future tenses have been explained in the conjugation of verbs. They are, for example, of the present tense, ക്ഷണംകൊണ്ടു കഴിഞ്ഞുപൊകുന്നകാലം, the time which passes quickly away, and this is formed by changing the final ഉ of the present into ന്ന, as പൊകുന്ന.

The preterite is formed from the pret. indicative which if it end in ഉ this is changed into ന്നി the letter യ is added except in the verbs പൊകുന്നു, and ആകുന്നു and its compounds, in which the final ി is changed in യ without adding it as ഞാൻസ്നെഹിച്ചപൈതൽമരിച്ചു the Boy whom I loved is dead; കട്ടുപൊയമുതൽവീണ്ടുകൊടുക്കയുംവെണം you must restore the stolen property, കഴിഞ്ഞുപൊയ വർഷകാലത്ത ആറ്റിലെവെള്ളംഎത്രയുംപൊങ്ങിപൊയി last winter the water of the River rose very much.

The future participle is compounded of the supine with the addition of the verb ഇരിക്കുന്നു; but, in speaking of a thing to happen at a great interval of time, we add ഉള്ളു, as വരു

[illegible] in the n[illegible] [illegible] I heard that your Highneſs is about to return in[to his] own coutry; [illegible] the Prophets believed in Chri[st] who was [to] come; [illegible] when the mother who was about to die ſaw her ſon ſhe became better, and in a few days recovered.

Here it ſhould be remembered, as was before obſerved in ſpeaking of the adjective, that theſe participles may become adjectives by placing them before the noun, as, [illegible] in the laſt war; [illegible] a withered tree; and by joining to them the pronouns [illegible], [illegible], [illegible] they may be declined as in the third Lecture reſpecting pronouns, as may be more fully ſeen.

LECTURE SIXTH,

Cauſal or Effective verbs.

What we expreſs in two verbs, the Malabars do by a ſingle word, which may be termed a cauſal or effective verb. Thus, to make to come, to cauſe to do, to make to love, are in Malabars ſingle expreſsions. But as theſe are formed in various modes according to the form of the radical verb, the following Rules are laid down for the more readily diſtinguiſhing the primary verb.

RULE

Verbs which ... more ... or cause by a ... കുന്നു love, ... to cause to love, pret. ... to labour, ... to make to call; ... to make laugh; ... to cause to take; കൈപ്പിക്കുന്നു to receive, ... to take to hear. ... to hear, കേൾ...

Exceptions,

... to sit, ... to cause to sit; ... stand, ... to make stand; ... to walk ... to make walk; ... to pass ... to pass; ... to lie down ... to make to lie; ... to cause ... to be appealed ... to make calm.

RULE SECOND.

The verb substantive, and its compounds, and verbs active in കുന്നു make their effectives by changing കുന്നു into ക്കുന്നു as ആകുന്നു to be, or have, ആക്കുന്നു to make to be, or have; ഉണ്ടാകുന്നു to have, ഉണ്ടാക്കുന്നു to make to have; പോകുന്നു to go പോക്കുന്നു to cause to go; ഒഴുകുന്നു to flow, ഒഴുക്കുന്നു to cause to flow; ഉരുകുന്നു to become liquid, ഉരുക്കുന്നു to make to melt; പഴകുന്നു to accustom, പഴക്കുന്നു to make familiar; and some others similar to these, but not all, for some verbs have no effective.

In

RULE FOURTH.

Verbs in രുന്നു change this termination in ർത്തുന്നു, or ക്കുന്നു, as, വളരുന്നു to increase, വളർത്തുന്നു to make grow ...; പകരുന്നു to be changed, പകർത്തുന്നു, ... to change, തകരുന്നു to be broken, തകർത്തുന്നു, or തകർക്കുന്നു to break; തീരുന്നു to be finished, തീർക്കുന്നു to finish ...; വരുന്നു to come വരുത്തുന്നു, ... to cause to come.

EXCEPT.

തരുന്നു to give to me, or you, തരിയിക്കുന്നു, ...

RULE FIFTH.

Verbs in റുന്നു double റ in to റ്റുന്നു, ആറുന്നു to become cool ആറ്റുന്നു to make cool ...; ഏറുന്നു to ascend ഏറ്റുന്നു to make to ascend, to raise up, ...; കരയേറുന്നു to climb, to land, കരയേറ്റുന്നു, ...; മാറുന്നു to be altered, മാറ്റുന്നു, ... to cause to change.

EXCEPT.

പെറുന്നു to bring forth, പെറിയിക്കുന്നു, ...

RULE SIXTH.

There are also a few active verbs in ...ിക്കുന്നു, or ...ക്കുന്നു; ... to cause &c. ... make to ...

വരുവാനുള്ളിരിക്കുന്ന കാലത്തിൽ in the next year; അങ്ങുന്നു രാജ്യത്തേക്ക് തിരിച്ചുപോകുവാനുള്ളിരിക്കുന്നു എന്നു കേട്ടു I heard that your Highneſs is about to return into your own coutry; വരുവാനുള്ളിരുന്ന ക്രിസ്തുനെ ദീർഘദർശിമാർ വിശ്വസിച്ചിരുന്നു the Prophets believed in Chriſt who was to come; മരിപ്പാനുള്ളിരുന്ന അമ്മ മകനെ കണ്ടാറെ ആശ്വാസം ആയി ചെന്നാറെ ചില ദിവസത്തിൽ ഭേദം വന്നും പൊറുത്തു when the mother who was about to die ſaw her ſon ſhe became better, and in a few days recovered.

Here it ſhould be remembered, as was before obſerved in ſpeaking of the adjective, that theſe participles may become adjectives by placing them before the noun, as, കഴിഞ്ഞപോരിൽ in the laſt war; ഉണങ്ങിപ്പോയ വൃക്ഷം a withered tree; and by joining to them the pronouns അവൻ, അവൾ, അത they may be declined as in the third Lecture reſpecting pronouns, as may be more fully ſeen.

LECTURE SIXTH,

Cauſal or Effective verbs.

What we expreſs in two verbs, the Malabars do by a ſingle word, which may be termed a cauſal or effective verb. Thus, to make to come, to cauſe to do, to make to love, are in Malabars ſingle expreſsions. But as theſe are formed in various modes according to the form of the radical verb, the following Rules are laid down for the more readily diſtinguiſhing the primary verb.

RULE

RULE FIRST.

Verbs which end in the present in ക്കുന്നു become effectives, or causals by adding പ്പി before ക്കുന്നു, for instance, സ്നേഹിക്കുന്നു I love, സ്നേഹിപ്പിക്കുന്നു to cause to love, pret. സ്നേഹിപ്പിച്ചു; പ്രയത്നിക്കുന്നു to labour, പ്രയത്നിപ്പിക്കുന്നു; വിളിക്കുന്നു to call, വിളിപ്പിക്കുന്നു to make to call; ചിരിക്കുന്നു to laugh, ചിരിപ്പിക്കുന്നു to make laugh; വാങ്ങിക്കുന്നു to receive, വാങ്ങിപ്പിക്കുന്നു to cause to take; കേൾക്കുന്നു to hear, കേൾപ്പിക്കുന്നു to make to hear.

Exceptions,

ഇരിക്കുന്നു to sit, ഇരുത്തുന്നു, ന്നി to cause to sit; നിൽക്കുന്നു to stand, നിറുത്തുന്നു to make stand; നടക്കുന്നു to walk നടത്തുന്നു, ന്നി to make walk; കടക്കുന്നു to pass കടത്തുന്നു, ന്നി to cause to pass; കിടക്കുന്നു to lie down കിടത്തുന്നു, ന്നി to make to lie; ശമിക്കുന്നു to be appeased ശമത്തുന്നു to make calm.

RULE SECOND.

The verb substantive, and its compounds, and verbs active in കുന്നു make their effectives by changing കുന്നു into ക്കുന്നു as ആകുന്നു to be, or have, ആക്കുന്നു to make to be, or have; ഉണ്ടാകുന്നു to have, ഉണ്ടാക്കുന്നു to make to have; പോകുന്നു to go പോക്കുന്നു to cause to go; ഒഴുകുന്നു to flow, ഒഴുക്കുന്നു to cause to flow; ഉരുകുന്നു to become liquid, ഉരുക്കുന്നു to make to melt; പഴകുന്നു to accustom, പഴക്കുന്നു to make familiar; and some others similar to these, but not all, for some verbs have no effective.

In

In the ſame manner, verbs in ങ്ങുന്നു are made effective by changing ങ്ങുന്നു into ക്കുന്നു, as മുങ്ങുന്നു to ſink മുക്കുന്നു to cauſe to ſink, മുക്കി; ഒങ്ങുന്നു to grow ripe, ഒക്കുന്നു, ക്കി to make ripe; വിങ്ങുന്നു to ſmother വിക്കുന്നു, വിക്കി; അടങ്ങുന്നു to be included, അടക്കുന്നു, ക്കി to include; കലങ്ങുന്നു to be diſturbed, കലക്കുന്നു to trouble water; നീങ്ങുന്നു to ritire നീക്കുന്നു, നീക്കി to take away; വെങ്ങുന്നു to be hot, വെക്കുന്നു to heat; മടങ്ങുന്നു to be conquered, മടക്കുന്നു to conquer.

RULE THIRD.

Verbs which have not the final ന്നു preceded by ക or ങ്ങ become cauſal by changing the ſyllable into ി and ending in ിക്കുന്നു ſo, തല്ലുന്നു to ſtrike തല്ലിക്കുന്നു to cauſe to ſtrike; ചെയ്യുന്നു to do ചെയ്യിക്കുന്നു to cauſe to do; പറയുന്നു to ſpeak, പറയിക്കുന്നു to make ſpeak; ചൊല്ലുന്നു to ſpeak, ചൊല്ലിക്കുന്നു to cauſe to ſpeak; വാഴുന്നു to reign, വാഴിക്കുന്നു to cauſe to reign.

Except the followiug,

തിന്നുന്നു to eat തീറ്റുന്നു, റ്റി to feed, ഉണ്ണുന്നു to eat rice ഊട്ടുന്നു to cauſe to eat rice; വീഴുന്നു to fall വീഴ്ത്തുന്നു to cauſe to fall or വീഴിക്കുന്നു, ച്ചു; കൂടുന്നു to be united, കൂട്ടുന്നു, ട്ടി to cauſe to join; വരുന്നു to come, വരുത്തുന്നു to make to come; നനയുന്നു to be wet നനക്കുന്നു to make wet; ഉരുളുന്നു to fly, ഉരുട്ടുന്നു, ട്ടി to make fly; കാണുന്നു to ſee, കാട്ടുന്നു to ſhew, ട്ടി; താഴുന്നു to be under, താഴ്ത്തുന്നു to put down; അണയുന്നു to approach, അണക്കുന്നു to make &c. ച്ചു; വാടുന്നു to wither as flowers വാട്ടുന്നു, ട്ടി to dry up.

RULE

RULE FOURTH.

Verbs in ഉന്നു change this termination in ത്തുന്നു, or ക്കുന്നു; as, വളരുന്നു to increase, വളൎത്തുന്നു to make grow ൎത്തി; പകരുന്നു to be changed, പകൎത്തുന്നു, ൎത്തി to change, തകരുന്നു to be broken, തകൎത്തുന്നു, or തകൎക്കുന്നു to break; തീരുന്നു to be finished, തീൎക്കുന്നു to finish ൎത്തു; വരുന്നു to come വരുത്തുന്നു, ത്തി to cause to come.

EXCEPT.

തരുന്നു to give to me, or you, തരിയിക്കുന്നു, ച്ചു.

RULE FIFTH.

Verbs in റുന്നു double റ in to റ്റുന്നു, ആറുന്നു to become cool ആറ്റുന്നു to make cool റ്റി; ഏറുന്നു to ascend ഏറ്റുന്നു to make to ascend, to raise up, ഏറ്റി; കരെയെറുന്നു to climb, to land, കരെയെറ്റുന്നു, റ്റി; മാറുന്നു to be altered, മാറ്റുന്നു, റ്റി to cause to change.

EXCEPT.

പെറുന്നു to bring forth, പെറിയിക്കുന്നു, ച്ചു.

RULE SIXTH.

There are also a few active verbs which are made effective in പ്പിക്കുന്നു, or യിക്കുന്നു; വളൎക്കുന്നു to educate വളൎപ്പിക്കുന്നു to cause &c. വളൎത്തു; തീൎക്കുന്നു to finish, തീൎപ്പിക്കുന്നു to make to finish ൎത്തു, കാട്ടുന്നു to shew, കാട്ടിക്കുന്നു, ച്ചു to cause to shew; ഏറ്റുന്നു to raise up ഏറ്റിക്കുന്നു, ച്ചു to make to raise.

LECTURE

LECTURE SEVENTH.

OF VERBS PASSIVE,

The Malabars ſeldom uſe the Paſſive voice, but ſince it is ſometimes employed, the rule is ſubjoined by which verbs active become paſſive; namely, by taking away the final ന്നു and changing the penultimate ഉ into ന, annexing the verb പെടുന്നു in this manner, സ്നേഹിക്കുന്നു to love, സ്നേഹിക്കപ്പെടുന്നു to be loved; ഘോഷിക്കുന്നു to celebrate, ഘോഷിക്കപ്പെടുന്നു to be celebrated, തുറക്കുന്നു to open തുറക്കപ്പെടുന്നു to be opened.

All verbs paſſive have the preterite ending in ട്ടു, and conjugated as in the 4th Lecture.

But it ſhould be remarked that ſome verbs cannot be made paſſive without the utmoſt impropriety, and ſolecism in language.

Secondly, that many verbs with the addition of പ്പെടുന്നു are not paſſive, but common, or active, or deponent, and are formed by joining പെടുന്നു to certain nouns only, for the greater number cannot be united with it, thus പ്രിയം love, makes പ്രിയപ്പെടുന്നു to love; സ്നേഹം love, സ്നേഹപ്പെടുന്നു to love; പീഡ pain പീഡപ്പെടുന്നു to ſuffer; നിന്ദം contempt, നിന്ദപ്പെടുന്നു to deſpiſe.

A paſſive mode of ſpeech is alſo formed from certain adverbs, as from ദൂരെ far, is made ദൂരെപ്പെടുന്നു to be diſtant;

അകം

അകം within, അകപ്പെടുന്നു to be enclosed; മെൽ above, മെല്പെടുന്നു to be over, to remain; hence മെൽ, or മെല്പെടുന്നവൻ a superior, tho' മെലവൻ is better.

LECTURE EIGHTH,

OF THE VERB PERSONAL.

It was before obſerved that all verbs in this language are impersonal. In poetry, however, and their beſt writings, we find a firſt, and third perſon ſingular, and a third perſon plural as.

Preſent ഞാൻചെയ്യിക്കുന്നേൻ, അവൻചെയ്യി ക്കുന്നാൻ, അവൾചെയ്യിക്കുന്നാൾ, അവർചെയ്യിക്കുന്നാർ.

Preterite ഞാൻചെയ്യിച്ചേൻ, അവൻചെയ്യിച്ചാൻ, അവൾചെയ്യിച്ചാൾ, അവർചെയ്യിച്ചാർ.

Future ഞാൻചെയ്യിപ്പേൻ, അവർചെയ്യിപ്പാർ.

no other tenſes are uſed, and theſe very ſparingly.

LECTURE NINTH.

OF IMPERFECT AND ANOMALOUS VERBS,

Irregular, or anomalous verbs are divided into two Claſſes; affirmative, and negative, and both require the perſon ſpoken of to be in the dative caſe.

The affirmatives are ഉണ്ട to be, or have, pres. എനിക്ക. നി നക്ക. ഉണ്ട I, or you have (eſt mihi).

But in other tenſes we muſt uſe the verb ഉണ്ടാകുന്നു; as,

എ

ഇരിക്കഉണ്ടായിരുന്നു I had; അവൎക്കഉണ്ടായി they had; നമുക്കഉണ്ടാകും we shall have.

This verb makes ഉള്ള in the participle, whence comes ഉള്ളവൻ. ഉള്ളവൾ. ഉള്ളത who, or which is. See farther in the section of adjectives; this verb has also another form in ഉള്ളു, which is *alone* or only.

But the verb, or noun preceding this must always end in എ, as, എത്രപേരഉണ്ട how many persons are there രണ്ടെ ഉള്ളു there are two only.

This defective verb is joined to almost all verbs, by changing ന്നു into ഉണ്ട; thus സ്നേഹിക്കുന്നുണ്ട I am loving; which form is also used for the future, as സ്നേഹിക്കുന്നുണ്ട I will love വരുന്നുണ്ട I come, or I will come.

But when we would use this verb in a past sense, we use the preterite in ഇട്ട, changing ട്ട into ട്ടു, and adding ണ്ട, as, സ്നേഹിച്ചിട്ടുണ്ട I was loving; അവൻവന്നിട്ടുണ്ട He came; or is come. We also use the verb ഉണ്ട when we would express the habit, or custom of doing a thing, substituting for the final ന്നു the termination കാറു ഉണ്ട, as, സ്നേഹിക്കാറുണ്ട I used to love; ചെയ്യുകാറുഉണ്ട I am accustomed to do; ചൊല്ലുകാറുഉണ്ട I am in the habit of saying.

Secondly വേണം I must, or will; Present എനിക്കവേണം, or വേണ്ടിയിരിക്കുന്നു, It is necessary for me, I must, or will, നിങ്ങൾക്കവേണ്ടിയിരിക്കുന്നു you wish, or must. pret. എനിക്ക; or നിങ്ങൾക്കവേണ്ടിയിരുന്നു; Future വേണ്ടിയിരിക്കും; Infin. വേണം എന്ന prerer.

Preter. വെണ്ടിരുന്നിരുന്നു; Part. വെണ്ടുന്നു, or വെണ്ടിയിരിക്കുന്നു; neuter വെണ്ടത, വെണ്ടുവത, or വെണ്ടിരിക്കുന്നത.

But observe, this verb may be joined to all others by removing the final ന, and changing the penultimate ഉ into എ long, thus ഏണം, as, സ്നെഹിക്കുന്നു makes സ്നെഹിക്കെണം I must love; വരുന്നു to come വരെണം I must come.

And that this may added, without change, to all verbs in the second singular imperative by adding thereto the letter യും, thus സ്നെഹിക്കയും വെണം you, or we must love, from സ്നെഹി love thou; പൊകയും വെണം from പൊക go; മൊക്ഷം നെടുവാൻ തമ്പുരാന്റെ കല്പന കാത്തു കൊൾകയും വെണം to aquire glory, or happiness, we must obey the law of God.

In place of the verb വെണം we may make use of വെണ്ടി, to which ഇരിക്കുന്നു is always joined, or sometimes വരുന്നു, thus വെണ്ടിരിക്കുന്നു, or വെണ്ടിവരുന്നു, I must, വെണ്ടിരുന്നു, or വെണ്ടിന്നു it was necessary. But to express the other tenses we ought to join to this defective verb, ഇരിക്കുന്നു or വരുന്നു in the tense required, as വെണ്ടിവന്നപ്പൊൾ when it was necessary; വെണ്ടിരിക്കുന്നെങ്കിൽ if it be necessary; വെണ്ടിവരുമ്പൊൾ when it shall be needful.

Sometimes also വെണ്ടി is made to coalesce with other verbs, as was said of വെണം, by changing the final ക of the imperative into എ long, with the addition of ണ്ടി and ഇരിക്കുന്നു, or വരുന്നു in that tense which the sense requires as പൊകെണ്ടിവരും it will be necessary for you to go; കൊള്ളി-

ക്കെ

ക്കുപൊകെണ്ടിവന്നു I was obliged to go to Cochin; നിന്നെത ല്ലെണ്ടിവരും I shall be forced to beat you.

Instead of വെണ്ടി, sometimes വെണ്ടു is added in the manner before said, which however gives the verb the force of a supine, as, കൊച്ചിക്കുപൊകെണ്ടുവന്നു I came in order to go to Cochin; മൊക്ഷംകിട്ടെണ്ടുപ്രായശ്ചിത്തം ചെയ്യുന്നു to acquire happiness I do penance.

Thirdly. The verb ആം I am able, this has only the present tense as, എനിക്കാം I can; അവക്കാം. It is joined to other verbs either entire, or contracted; in the first case the verb is in the imperative in ക with യും annexed, as in the case of വെണം, thus, സ്നെഹിക്കയും ആം, only that the final ം is changed into its corresponding vocal consonant, and it is written മാം, thus പൊകയുമാം I can go; ഉണ്ണ്കയുമാം I can eat rice; this only in the instances where the imperative ends in ക, or ക്ക; if it has a different termination, then the final ന്നു of the present is dropped, and കയുമാം is added instead; thus, ചൊല്ലുകയുമാം I can say; തൂക്കുകയുമാം I can suspend; which is also to be observed when this sort of verbs precedes വെണം.

When this verb is contracted with the preceding, it is done by adding, tothe second person of the imperative, the particle ആം, or if you please, by changing the termination ക്കും the future into ആം, thus സ്നെഹിക്കാം I can love, from സ്നെഹിക്ക the imperative, or സ്നെഹിക്കും the future; ചൊല്ലാം I can speak,

speak, from ചൊല്ലു, or ചൊല്ലും; this verb may be traced perhaps to the substantive verb ഉണ്ടു as its origin.

In the same manner we use the defective അറിയാം only in the present, it signifies either I know, or I know not, from അറിയുന്നു to know.

Fourthly. മതി it is enough; എനിക്കുമതി it suffices for me; it is used only in the present. When other tenses are required they are formed by the aid of the verb ഉണ്ടു I am, as മതിയായി it was sufficient; മതിയാകും it will suffice മതിയാകും ചൊല്ലുവിൻ; speak when there shall be enough.

The opposite correspondent to this verb മതി is പോരാ it is not enough, as എനിക്കുപോരാ. പോരാഞ്ഞു it is, or was not enough or me; Part പോരാത്ത which is not sufficient, from which comes the substantive പോരായ്ക insufficiency.

Of Imperfect Negative Verbs.

First. വേണ്ട I will not, I do not want, I need not. Present എനിക്കുവേണ്ട I want not; Prete. വേണ്ടാഞ്ഞു, 2d. വേണ്ടാഞ്ഞാൽ, 3d വേണ്ടാഞ്ഞിട്ടു, 4th. വേണ്ടാഞ്ഞാറെ because I was unwilling or wanted not.

Inf. വേണ്ടെന്നു; Pret. വേണ്ടാഞ്ഞെന്നു, വേണ്ടാഞ്ഞിട്ടെന്നു; noun substantive വേണ്ടായ്ക inconvenience, uselessness.

This verb is joined to others by taking away ഉന്നു, and substituting എണ്ട as, സ്നേഹിക്കേണ്ട I will not, I need not love; ചെയ്യേണ്ട you must not, or should not do. But this

this form of expression is more commonly used in the imperative mood, as പൊകൊല്ല do not go; കരയൊല്ല do not weep; വരൊല്ല you must not come.

Second. ഇല്ല, or അല്ല not to be, or have as; എനിക്കഇല്ല I have not. Pret. ഇല്ലാഞ്ഞു. 2d, ഇല്ലാഞ്ഞാൽ 3d. ഇല്ലാഞ്ഞിട്ട. 4th. ഇല്ലാഞ്ഞാലെ.

Inf. ഇല്ലയെന്നു; or ഇല്ലെന്നു Pret. ഇല്ലാഞ്ഞയെന്നു; Part. ഇല്ലാത്ത which is not; Pret. ഇല്ലാഞ്ഞ; Supine ഇല്ലായ്കയാൽ; Noun substantive ഇല്ലായ്മ want; as ബുദ്ധിഇല്ലായ്മകൊണ്ടഇതവന്ന this happened for want of Judgement.

It is to be observed, first that അല്ല is declined in the same manner as above, with the difference of the first letter, as അല്ലാഞ്ഞിട്ട. അല്ലാത്ത &ca.

2dly. We use the present participles of these verbs to form negative adjectives, and also substantives with the addition of അവൻ, അവൾ, അത as observed in the lecture on the adjectives.

This verb is joined to verbs affimative in order to give them a negative sense; in this case the final ഉ is omitted, and ഇ added instead, thus, ചെയ്യുന്നില്ല; Pret. ചെയ്തില്ല; ചെയ്തിട്ടില്ല Fut. ചെയ്കയില്ല; or ചെയ്കില്ല; പൊകില്ല I will not go. Whence it appears that, when ഇല്ല is joined to the future, the final ഉം is cut off, or exchanged for ഇല്ല, thus, it is not written വരുംഇല്ല,

But

But, വരില്ല; not തല്ലുംഇല്ല, But തല്ലില്ല I will not beat.

But when a negative is required to be joined to the imperative mood അല്ല is used instead of ഇല്ല, as സ്നേഹിക്കല്ല, or സ്നേഹിക്കല്ലായെ

In this manner ഇല്ല may be joined to all verbs which then require a dative of the person, unless the verb, requires by its nature, a different case.

From this verb is formed മനസ്സില്ല, to which is opposed മനസ്സുണ്ട I am willing. (see Primitive Negative adverbs.

Thirdly അരുത, I cannot ഇരിക്കരുത; Pret. അരുതാഞ്ഞു; 2d. അരുതാഞ്ഞാൽ; 3d. അരുതാഞ്ഞിട്ട; 4th. അരുതാഞ്ഞാറെ when, after that, I could not.

Inf. അരുതായ്കകൊണ്ട; Pret. അരുതാഞ്ഞുകൊണ്ട; Part. അരുതാത്ത which cannot; Pret. അരുതാഞ്ഞ Noun substantive അരുതായ്മ Inability.

When this verb is joined to others ഉക is changed for അരുത, thus ചെയ്യരുത I cannot do; സ്നേഹിക്കരുത I cannot love, പൊകരുത I cannot go.

But when, as is sometimes the case, it is added without any alteration, the preceding verb is made to end in കയും, (in the same manner as explained in the words ഏറും, പെറും) and അരുത is annexed to this termination; thus പൊകയും അരുത I cannot go; നടക്കയും അരുത I cannot walk, പറകയും അരുത I cannot speak.

Fourthly. വയ്യ I am unable, which may be conjugated

gated like അരുത, but it is seldom used unless in the present tense, as ഇനിക്കൊല്ലാ I cannot, ഇതിനിക്കൊല്ലാ I cannot do this, സ്നേഹിപ്പാനൊല്ലാ I cannot love, ചെയ്വാനൊല്ലാ I cannot do, ഇനിക്കവിശ്വസിപ്പാനൊല്ലാ I cannot believe it.

Fifthly. വഹിയാ I cannot, is also conjugated in the same manner as above, with a dative of the person, ഇനിക്കവഹിയാ; Pret വഹിയാഞ്ഞു, Inf. വഹിയായ്ക; Part വഹിയാത്ത; neuter, വഹിയാത്തത which cannot be.

When joined with other verbs, these ought to be in the supine, as with ഒല്ലാ; thus തിന്മാൻവഹിയാ I cannot eat; നടപ്പാൻവഹിയാ I cannot walk.

Sixthly. കൂടാ, I am unable, is conjugated in the same manner, thus കൂടാ; Pret. കൂടാഞ്ഞു; കൂടാഞ്ഞാൻ; കൂടാഞ്ഞിട്ട Inf. കൂടായ്ക, Pret. കൂടാഞ്ഞയ്ക; Part. കൂടാത്ത; neuter കൂടാത്തത, like വേണ്ടാത്തത, പാടില്ലാത്തത, ഇല്ലാത്തത.

This verb is joined, without any change, to the preterite of others; it requires a dative ഇനിക്കചെയ്തുകൂടാ I cannot do it; ഇനിക്കപോയികൂടാ I cannot go. അവന്ക്കുവന്നുകൂടാ he cannot come.

It is proper for Learners to write all the defective verbs with *a* long, as കൂടാ, പാടില്ലാ, വഹിയാ, ഇല്ലാ.

Besides these defective verbs, which joined to regulars make a negative signification, there are certain particles which have the same power, such are ഏ and ഏകെ.

Of

Of the Negative particle ആ

All verbs become negative, if, in place of the final ഉന്നു, you annex ആ, as, 1st. Pret. ചെയ്യാത്തു, or ചെയ്യാഞ്ഞു, 2d Pret. ചെയ്യാഞ്ഞാൽ by not doing, or having done; 3d. ചെയ്യാഞ്ഞിട്ട്; Inf. ചെയ്യായ്വാൻ; Pret. ചെയ്യാത്തെയ്വാൻ; Part. ചെയ്യാത്ത; Supine ചെയ്യായ്വാൻ; noun ſubſtantive, ചെയ്യായ്ക.

So alſo വരാ, he comes not, Pret. വരാത്തു; or വരാഞ്ഞു; വരാഞ്ഞാൽ: വരാഞ്ഞിട്ട്; Part. വരാത്ത, neuter വരാത്തത്; Supine വരായ്വാൻ; noun Substantive വരായ്ക the not coming, the non arrival·

In the ſame manner is conjugated പോകാ I cannot go; നടക്കാ I cannot walk. From which it might appear that this mode of expreſſion is deducible from വേണ്ട, or കൂടാ.

Affirmative verbs, alſo, become negative, by the additiuo of the particle ആതെ, inſtead of ഉന്നു, and by joining to this, ഇരിക്കുന്നു, in whatever tenſe the ſentence may require, thus from സ്നേഹിക്കുന്നു is formed, സ്നേഹിക്കാതെഇരിക്കുന്നു I do not love, from പറയുന്നു to ſpeak, പറയാതെഇരിക്കുന്നു he is ſilent, പോകാതെഇരിക്കുന്നു he will not go.

Sometimes by way of adding grace, or elegance to the expreſſion, കണ്ടു is joined to ആതെ, thus പറയാതെകണ്ടിരുന്നു he was ſilent, or ſpoke not·

Sometimes alſo a verb ending in ആതെകണ്ടു is joined with other verbs, and in this caſe it may be rendered by our expreſſion

preſſion without being, as നനയാതെവന്നു I came without being wet, അറിയാതെചെയ്തു I did it without knowing; പറയാതെകണ്ടുകടന്നുപൊയി He went away without ſpeaking.

More will be ſaid on this ſubject when treating of adverbs to which the reader is referred for fuller information.

LECTURE TENTH.

Of Verbs of Elegance,

This ſort of verbs is uſed by the Malabarians to add force, or beauty to an expreſſion. They are as follows; കൊള്ളുന്നു to buy, to take, or receive, is joined to the preterite of verbs, and ſeems to have no other ſenſe than to mark the time, or tenſe, for the preceding verb expreſſes the ſignification, which is alſo the caſe with other emphatical, or ornamental verbs, as മനുഷ്യർപിഴച്ചതിന്റെശെഷം തമ്പുരാന്റെപുത്രൻ അവരെരക്ഷിച്ചുകൊണ്ടു after that men had ſinned the ſon of God redeemed them, ഞാനാകുംവണ്ണംപറഞ്ഞുകൊണ്ടു നീകെട്ടില്ലയൊ I told you all I could, did you not hear?

Secondly. കളയുന്നു to caſt out, is added to verbs in the preterite, as, പൊയികളഞ്ഞു he departed; പൊയികളയും he will go; ഇറക്കികളയുന്നു to turn out; തല്ലികളയുന്നു to beat, തല്ലിക്കളഞ്ഞു Preterite.

Thirdly. ഇരിക്കുന്നു to exiſt, to be, to ſit, is joinedteo the

the preterite also, thus സ്നേഹിച്ചിരിക്കുന്നു I am loving, അവൻ ഇതുപറഞ്ഞിരിക്കുമ്പോൾ when he is saying this, എഴുതിയിരിക്കുന്നപോലെ as it is written.

Fourthly. കിടക്കുന്നു, to lie, is also added to the preterite, as ചൊല്ലിക്കിടക്കുന്നു it is said, എഴുതിക്കിടക്കുന്നു it is written.

Fifthly. അയക്കുന്നു to send, is joined to the same tense, only the initial അ is cut off, & it is written യക്കുന്നു, and preterites ending in ഉ are changed into അ, but those in യി remain unchanged, thus, ഇതവനോടുപറഞ്ഞെയച്ചിട്ടുപുറപ്പെട്ടുപോയി when he had said this to him he departed.

Sixthly. വിടുന്നു to dismiss, when added to the preterite of a verb signifies to send, as ചൊല്ലിവിടുന്നു I send to say, or ചൊല്ലൂടുന്നു, preterite ചൊല്ലൂട്ടു. കൊടുത്തുവിടുന്നു to send to give; this is commonly written കൊടുത്തൂടുന്നു, Pret. കൊടുത്തൂട്ടു.

In the same manner തന്നുവിടുന്നു to send to give (speaking of the 1st. or 2d. person) or തന്നൂടുന്നു pret. തന്നൂട്ടു. hence it appears that വിടുന്നു in composition is written, and pronounced as if it was ഊടുന്നു, But this form is very seldom used and only in the above examples.

Seventhly, തരുന്നു to give to the first, or second person; കൊടുക്കുന്നു to give to the third, being joined to the preterite, add somewhat to the signification of the verb; എടുത്തുതന്നു he took, and gave it me ചൊല്ലിതന്നു he gave me in words, or or he said to me; പഠിപ്പിച്ചുകൊടുത്തു he taught him, gave instruction,

Eighthly ചെയ്യുന്നു to do, may be joined to other verbs in three different ways.

1st. To the Imperative, in which case ചെയ്യുന്നു is used in the participle of the present, or preter tense, as അവൻ പഠിക്കചെയ്യുന്നു he teaches; ഇന്നലെവരികചെയ്തു he came yesterday.

2dly. the particle ഉം is annexed to the imperative, and ചെയ്യുന്നു, and ചെയ്തു is added in the same manner as വേണം, and ഉണ്ടു; thus, അവൻ വരികയുംചെയ്തു he came; ഞാൻ പെരികെ സന്തൊഷിക്കയുംചെയ്തു I am much rejoiced; and not unfrequently it governs two, or three verbs, as in the following example, വെണ്ടുംവണ്ണംകുമ്പസാരിക്കയുംഒരു ഷമിക്കെ മനസ്താപപ്പെടുകയും ഇനിമെൽപാവിഷക്കളല്ലു ന്നകന്നിരിക്കയുംചെയ്യുന്നവർക്കൊരുപെരുക്കിട്ടും. They who do truly confess, and repent of their sins, and resolve to trangress no more shall obtain remission of their sins.

This form of speech is very common.

3dly. The last way in which this verb is annexed to others, is to the supine, dropping the final *an* ആൻ, and substituting, ഊതും E. G. ഒന്നാമത്തെ മനുഷ്യൻ വിലക്കിയ കായിതിന്നുതും ചെയ്തിട്ടു ശിക്ഷക്ക യൊഗ്യനായ്പൊതും ചെയ്തു The first man by eating the forbiden fruit made himself liable to punishment; അവൻ അതുചെയ്യപ്പൊതും ചെയ്തു He did

did it; from which laſt example, it is plain that, this verb may be added, in the manner aforeſaid, to itſelf.

Ninthly. വരുന്നു, to come, is joined to the verb വെണ്ടു; as, വെണ്ടിവരും it will be neceſſary. It is added alſo to verbs which have this defective verb previouſly annexed to them, as, പൊകെണ്ടിവരും I ſhall be forced to go; to this verb വെണ്ടു is alſo added ഇരിക്കുന്നു, as വെണ്ടിരിക്കുന്നു it will be neceſſary,

See the paragraph on വെണം above:

Tenthly. ഇരിക്കുന്നു to be, is added to the imperative, അവൻ അതു പറെക്കിരിക്കുന്നു he ſaid ſo; അവൻ അതു ചെയ്തിരിക്കുന്നു he did it.

Eleventhly. ചമെയുന്നു to become, is joined to the preterites of the verbs ഇരിക്കുന്നു, and പൊകുന്നു; as പൊയിചമെഞ്ഞു he departed; മാലാഖമാര പാപംചെയ്തിട്ടു പിശാചുകളായിചമെഞ്ഞു the angels having ſinned became Devils.

LECTURE ELEVENTH.

Of the other Parts of ſpeech.

After having ſeparately treated of the noun, pronoun, verb, and participle, it remains to conſider the other parts of ſpeech as they regard ſyntax, or conſtruction. Namely, prepoſitions, the rules for forming the different caſes of the noun, adverbs, interjections, and conjunctions, from the combination

combination of all which the ſtructure of language is raiſed and fixed.

Of the Nominative.

This is placed before the verb not only in the definite moods, but alſo in the Infinitive, before participles ſimple, and compound, before ſubſtantives, and even ſupines. Ex. gr. താൻവരുമെന്നുകെട്ടു I heard you would come; അവൻവരുവാൻനിന്റെയപ്രയത്നം ചെയ്തെന്നുകെട്ടു I heard you uſed much diligence that he ſhould come; ഞാൻ അയച്ചവനെശത്രുകൊന്നു the enemy killed him whom I ſent; ഞാൻനന്നാക്കിയഅകത്തുടനാജ്ഞാവടക്കി the Raja has ſeized the houſe which I repaired.

Obſerve that, in neuter nouns, the nominative is uſed frequently; and generally, for the accuſative caſe, eſpecially in the Plural.

Secondly that, the adverb എല്ലാം all, every, takes a nominative before it; കാലംഎല്ലാം at all times; ആണ്ടെല്ലാം every year; എല്ലാട്ടംഎല്ലാംവെറ്റിലനാടെല്ലാംഭാഷ In every garden there is beetle leaf, and in every country a (different) language. Proverb.

Of the Genitive

When there is no rule to the contrary, the genitive is uſed as in the European languages; കുതിരെടെഉടെയവൻ the maſter of the horſe; നാട്ടിലെരാജാവ the king of the

country;

country; ആദിത്യന്റെവെളിവ the light of the sun; ഭൂമിയുടെവലിപ്പം the magnitnde of the Earth; മാൎഗ്ഗത്തിന്റെപ്രകാരം the ordonnance af the Law.

Observe 1st, that, nouns ending in ട double this letter into ട്ട, and so obtain the force of a genitive, thus from ചുമട a burden, and ആൾ a person, comes ചുമട്ടാൾ a bearer of burdens, a porter; from നാട a country, and ഛിദ്രം dissension, comes നാട്ടഛിദ്രം civil discord, the ട്ട being sometimes changed into ട്ടു, and, indeed, sometimes into ട്ടും, as ആട്ടുംപൂട sheep's wool.

Secondly. That, when two names of irrationals come together, one requiring in our idiom to be in the genitive, the Malabars leave it in the nominative, as പള്ളിതാക്കോൽ, to which the English has a corresponding expression, 'the Church key;' പള്ളിവാതിൽ the Church door; എരുമപ്പാൽ Buffalo's milk; കത്തോപ്പുര a harbour, or place where boats are laid up; വാഴയില a plaintain leaf. But this form of expression is not universal, and would often be absurd; thus we cannot say പാംപുപല്ല a serpent's tooth, നാടകലഹം a disturbance in a country; but പാംപിന്റെപല്ല; നാട്ടിന്റെകലഹം, or നാട്ടിലെകലഹം,

In general, when a noun ends in *a* short, it is safer for beginners to use always the genitive, rather than the nominative, until experience shall have taught them in what instances this peculiarity of expression may be used.

Thirdly

3 dly. nouns in ം must always be used in this sense in the genitive, so that you can never say മരംഇല, but മരത്തിൻ ഇല the leaf of a tree; ആകാശത്തിൻകൊമ്പ the celestial horn, or Cornucopia; വൃക്ഷത്തിന്റെകൊമ്പ the branch of a tree; ആകാശത്തിലെരാജാവ the king of Heaven, of the firmament, or skies

But they are sometimes put in the nominative, by cutting the final ം, and connecting the noun with the following one as മര തൊല the Bark of a tree; സമുദ്ര നീര് Sea water

See foregoing observations on the formation of adjectives where two substantives come in this manner together. But this form can never be used when the last noun begins with a vowel.

4 thly. that, nouns singnifying supreme authority, tho', they may be used in the genitive, are frequently put in the dative case, as രാജാക്കന്മാൎക്കുകീഴടങ്ങിയിരിക്കേണം we ought to be subject to kings; ഈകണ്ടത്തിന്ന ഉടയവൻ ഞാൻ I am master of this field; അവൎക്കുരാജാവുതമ്പുരാൻ your highness is their king; സിംഹംമൃഗങ്ങൾക്കുരാജാവാകുന്നു the Lion is the King of Beasts; ശാസ്ത്രത്തിന്ന ഉടമസ്ഥൻ അവൻ He is master of arts.

Prepositions which require a Genitive.

In the Malabar language these parts of speech are always placed after the noun; their more appropriate appellation would therefore be post positions, the following govern

govern the genitive case; അരികെ near, or അരിയത്ത, as പൊഴെടെഅരിയത്ത near the river, വീട്ടിന്റെഅരികെ near the house.

It requires also a dative as പള്ളിക്കരികെ.

അകത്ത within, പള്ളിയുടെഅകത്ത within the church;

Also sometimes a dative as പള്ളിക്കകത്ത.

അങ്ങെ beyond, ഇങ്ങെ on this side, and their compounds അങ്ങക്കരെ; ഇങ്ങക്കരെ; as പൊഴെടെഅങ്ങക്കരെ on that side of the river, and the latter sometimes with a dative, as പൊഴെക്കിങ്ങക്കരെ.

അങ്ങപ്പുറം beyond, ഇങ്ങപ്പുറം on this side, are adverbs, as ഞാൻഇങ്ങെപ്പുറത്തഅവൻഅങ്ങെപ്പുറത്തായിരുന്നു I was on this side, he on that.

എതിരെ, or നെരെ opposite; as പള്ളിയുടെനെരെ, or എതിരെ opposite the Church.

മെലെ, മെല്, or മീതെ over, upon, above; എന്റെമെലെ above me ഇതിന്റെമീതെ above this.

മുന്നെ, മുന്നിൽ, മുമ്പെ, or മുമ്പിൽ before, in presence of, എന്റെമുമ്പിൽ before me; നിന്റെമുമ്പാകെ before you;

പുറകെ, or പിറകെ behind, എന്റെപിറകെ behind me.

Also the adverbs അവിടെ, and ഇവിടെ there, here, require a genitive; as, നാട്ടിന്റെഎവിടെനീപാർക്കുന്നു where in the

the country do you live? ഞങ്ങടെ ഇവിടെ ഞെരുക്കം ഇല്ല here amongst us there is no disturbance; നിങ്ങടവിടെ നെല്ലു ഉണ്ടൊ is there any nelly (rice) with you?

Their compounds also require the same case, അവിടെനിന്നു from thence ഇവിടെനിന്നു, എവിടെനിന്നു, as; എന്റെ ഇവിടെനിന്നു വന്നു I came from my house; പെങ്ങളുടെ അവിടെക്കു പൊകുന്നു I go to my sister's house; തിരുമുമ്പിൽ, or തിരുമുമ്പാകെ before God, or the King.

But when മുമ്പെ or മുമ്പിൽ signifies the time past, then, the noun is better in the dative, as, വെനിൽക്കുമുമ്പെ before the summer; മഴെക്കുമുമ്പെ before the rains.

മുഖത്ത, or മുമ്പാകെ in presence of, governs a genitive, എന്റെ മുഖത്തു തല്ലി he struck him in my presence.

വക്കൽ to, or at. അവന്റെ വക്കൽ at him, to him; നിന്റെ വക്കൽ ചൊല്ലുവാൻ he sent to speak to you.

വഴി, വഴിയായി വഴിയായിട്ടു or, വഴിയെ according to, tho' included in those adverbs which require a genitive case, are more properly joined to the indeclinable noun in ത്തും; as, ന്യായത്തുംവഴി agreeable to justice; ദൊഷത്തുംവഴിയായി sinfully.

പിമ്പെ after, as സുഖത്തിന്റെ പിമ്പെ ദുഃഖം after mirth comes sorrow.

പുറത്ത upon, എന്റെ പുറത്തു വീണു he fell upon me; പള്ളിയുടെ പുറത്ത, or, with a dative പള്ളിക്കപുറത്ത without the church.

തി

കീഴു കീഴ beneath; also താഴെ, or താഴത്തു under; രാജാവിന്റെ താഴെ, or കീഴ under the Raja, സമുദ്രത്തിന്റെ താഴെ മണൽ the sand under the sea.

ശെഷം after, as അതിന്റെ ശെഷം after that.

ചുറ്റും about, as ഭൂമിയുടെ ചുറ്റും കടൽ the sea is round about the Earth.

Of the Dative

All verbs signifying gain, or loss, or injury, or the value of any thing, also verbs of going, such as imply the limit of motion to a place, verbs of giving, of buying, lending, shewing also the verbs substantive ആകുന്നു to be, കിട്ടുന്നു to acquire, ചെരുന്നു to fit, എത്തുന്നു to arrive, or reach at, require a dative case, as എനിക്ക ഉപകാരം ഉണ്ടായില്ല I gained nothing, അവൎക്ക വളരെ ചെതം വന്നു they suffered great loss; ശത്രുവിന്റെ ജയം ഉണ്ടായി the enemy gained the victory; എനിക്ക ബഹുമാനം നിണക്ക അബഹുമാനമാകെടവരും I shall have the honor, you the disgrace; സൎവ്വെശ്വരന്ന സ്തുതി praise be to God; മക്കൾക്ക അപ്പൻ ദ്രവ്യം വെക്കുന്നു the Father preserves money for his chidren.

Verbs which signify the boundary at which we would arrive; നഗരത്തിന പൊയി he went to the city; ആകാശത്തുക്കു കരെറിപ്പൊയി he ascended into Heaven; വെള്ളത്തിന്നപൊയി he went to the well, or tank; വിയാധി, or വ്യാധിക്ക ചികിത്സ ചെയ്യുന്നു he administers medicine for sickness.

But observe, when we say we go home, the dative is not used

used but the ablative in ഇൽ as ഞാൻവീട്ടിൽപൊകുന്നു I am going home; നരകത്തിൽപൊയി he went to Hell; മൊക്ഷത്തിൽപൊയി he went to heaven.

Of buying, and giving, as ഒരുപണത്തിനമുട്ടഇരുപതു twenty eggs (are bought) for a fanam; അവൻഎനിക്കഒരുപുസ്തകംതന്നുഞാൻപത്തുപണംഅവനുകൊടുത്തു He gave me a book, and I gave him ten fanams; ആയിരംപണംഎനിക്കവായിപ്പതരിക Lend me a thousand fanams; നൂറുഉറുപ്പികപലിശക്കകൊടുത്തു I lent at interest a hundred Rupees; എനിക്കനല്ലരൂപംകാട്ടുക shew me a fine image, or statue; എനിക്കസന്തൊഷമായി I had satisfaction, or joy.

The verb കിട്ടുന്നു; as നല്ലവർക്കമൊക്ഷംകിട്ടും the good shall obtain happiness, or heaven.

ചെരുന്നു to become, as നീചെയ്തതനിനക്കചെരുന്നില്ല what you have done does not become you, അടുക്കുന്നു to approach, as തീക്കഅടുത്താൽചുടും by going near to fire you will be burnt.

Secondly, The definitive verbs, as has been seen, require a dative case, but the verbs വെണം and വെണ്ട, when the person is absolutely necessary take the nominative, as, നിന്നെസ്തുതിവെണം you deserve praise; ഞാൻതന്നെഇക്കാര്യത്തിന്നുവെണം I myself am required in this business; നിന്നെസഹായിപ്പാൻവെണ്ട you are not wanted to help me; നീകൊച്ചിക്കപൊകെണം you must go to Cochin; നീപൊകെണ്ട you must not go.

The

The verb ഉണ്ടാകുന്നു requires a dative as observed of ആകുന്നു to be; ആം, and അരുത as also their compounds require the dative case. But when ആം signifies only a readiness to do a thing then it has a nominative; as, താങ്കൾകല്പിച്ചാൽ ഞാൻപൊകാം at your command I will go; In the same manner when അരുത signifies a refusal of assent in the way of a request not to do a thing, the person is put in the nominative, as നീപൊകരുത you must not go; താങ്കൾഇങ്ങനെ പറയരുത you must not say so.

The verb ഉണ്ട when it signifies to exist, or live takes the nominative, as രാജാവ ഉണ്ട കഴിഞ്ഞില്ല the Raja is living, he is not dead.

Likewise the compounds of ഉണ്ട, and ഇല്ല require the nominative, (although the simple verbs govern the dative case) as ദൈവകൃപയാൽ ഞാൻ ഒരുനാളും വീഴുകയില്ല by the help of God I shall never fall, നീ പറഞ്ഞത ഞാൻ കെൾക്കണ്ട I ought not to hear what you said.

The verbs കൂടാ, വേല, കഴിവില also require a dative case but their compounds which end in *a* long, in ആവു, or ആക will have the nominative; ഇന്ന ഇത ഞാൻ ചെയ്തുകൂടാ I cannot do this to day; ഞാൻ പറഞ്ഞത നീ കെൾക്കാഞ്ഞത എന്ത why did you not hear what I said?

Prepositions which govern the dative.

ഒക്കവണ്ണം, or ഒക്കപ്പോലെ according to; തക്കവണ്ണം, or തക്കപോലെ the same; വേണ്ടി, or വേണ്ടീട്ട because of;

പകരം

പകരം or പകരമായിട്ട instead of; തക്ക or തക്കത suitable to, or proportioned to; കിഴക്ക eastward, or കിഴക്കൊട്ട; തെക്ക, or തെക്കൊട്ട southward; വടക്ക, or വടക്കൊട്ട on the north. പടിഞ്ഞാറെ westward, or in the west; അകത്ത, or അകം within ഒരുമാസത്തിനകം, or അകത്ത within a month; Ex. Gr. In return for the favor you did me to the northward, I, also having gone into the south, when I had adopted means proportioned to the business of which you spoke, within two months time, effected the business according to your wish ഇനിക്കവെണ്ടിട്ടുവടക്കൊട്ട കാൎയ്യംചെയ്തു ഉപകാരത്തിന പകരമായിട്ടുഞാനും തെക്കൊട്ടുപൊയ്യാറെ കാൎയ്യംപറഞ്ഞകാൎയ്യത്തിനുതക്കഉപദെശങ്ങളെചിട്ടപ്പെടുത്തപ്പൊൾരണ്ടുമാസത്തിനകത്തകത്തവണ്ണംകാൎയ്യംസാധിക്കയുംചെയ്തു.

Of the Accusative.

All verbs active, and verbs signifying help, require an accusative of the thing, as ഇനിക്കുതുണെക്കതമ്പുരാനെ help me O God! തമ്പുരാൻമനുഷ്യരെസ്നെഹിക്കുന്നു God loves mankind.

All verbs which from active become effective require two accusatives, one of the person another of the thing as അവനെ മാൎഗ്ഗംകൂട്ടിച്ചു he caused him to enter into the Law; അനസ്താസിയൊസ്പാതിരി എന്നെ ശാസ്ത്രം പഠിപ്പിച്ചു the Father Anastasius taught me science.

Here it must be remembered that in neuter nouns the nominative serves for the accusative, which is to be particularly

larly noticed, and 2dly. that, to avoid confusion in effective verbs, we put the person, who is made to act, in the accusative governed by കൊണ്ടു, which is equivalent nearly to the particle *by*. മിടുക്കുള്ളവനെക്കൊണ്ടു ശത്രുവിനെ കൊല്ലിച്ചു I caused the enemy to be killed by a bold man 3dly. that verbs which end in ഊട്ടുന്നു and those which are compounded of വിടുന്നു to send, require an Acc. case of the person sent, with കൊണ്ടു, thus അവനെക്കൊണ്ടു ചൊല്ലിച്ചു I sent by him to speak to you; but sometimes for കൊണ്ടു they use the adverb വശാൽ as അവന്റെ വശാൽ പുസ്തകം കൊടുത്തയച്ചു I sent the Book by him 4. thly that participles, and nouns require the cases of the verbs from which they are derived; ദൈവത്തെ സ്നേഹിക്കുന്നവൻ a lover of God, ദൈവത്തെ ഉള്ള സ്നേഹം the love of God;

Prepositions requiring the Accusative.

ഇതാ Behold· ഞാനിതാ behold here I am; കുറിച്ച, കുറിച്ചു, കുറിച്ചിട്ടു, because of; മേൽ, മേലും, മേലാൽ; മേലിലും, മേട്ടിലും upon; കൊണ്ടു with or by

It sometimes signifies of, as, എന്നെക്കുറിച്ചു ദൂഷണം പറഞ്ഞു he spoke ill of me, and sometimes on account of, as, ഇതിനെക്കൊണ്ടു on this account; it is written also കൊണ്ടിട്ടു, as അവനെക്കൊണ്ടിട്ടു on his account; കൂടാതെ without, besides പോലെ like; as, അവനെപ്പോലെ എനിക്കു നടന്നുകൂടാ I cannot walk like him.

These prepositions in general require an accusative proper

But

But in neuter nouns the nominative is ſometimes uſed for it.

Of the Vocative

There are ſome prepoſitions, altho' they may be called as properly interjections, which govern the vocative caſe, as ഹെടാ O ſir! ഹെടൊ O you! ഹെടി (to a female); അയ്യൊ oh! expreſsive of pain, or grief, അയ്യൊ പാവിയെ oh wretch! അയ്യൊ ദുഷ്ടരെ perverse, or cruel men? അയ്യൊ സങ്കടമെ my complaint! അയ്യൊ oh; അയ്യൊ പിടിയാത്തവനെ ah unfit perſon! ഓ O! as, ഓ തമ്പുരാനെ O God! എന്റപ്പച്ചാ oh my Father.

Of the Ablative in ഇൽ,

Firſt, This caſe is always uſed to correſpond with our prepoſition *in*.

Secondly, The verbs പൂകുന്നു, and its effective പൂകിക്കുന്നു to cauſe to enter, require the ablative in ഇൽ, as പള്ളിയിൽ പൂകി he went into the Church, വേദത്തിൽ പൂകിച്ചു he made him enter into the Law. Yet ſometimes theſe verbs take an accuſative.

Thirdly, The verb പൊകുന്നു to go, and വരുന്നു to come very frequently governs this ablative in ഇൽ, as വീട്ടിൽ വന്നപ്പൊൾ when I came home.

Fourthly, The verb കൂടുന്നു to meet together, and its effective കൂട്ടുന്നു to collect together, take the ablative in ഇൽ, alſo the verbs ഏറുന്നു to aſcend, and കയറുന്നു with its effective കയറ്റുന്നു to make to aſcend.

Fifthly,

Fifthly, The ablative ഇൽ is used in comparison, as ഭൂമിയിൽ വല്യതു കടൽ the sea is larger than the Earth. also when in comparing, or reckoning, we would express the sense of *among* it is used as ഈ പണങ്ങളിൽ ഒന്നും നല്ലതില്ല of or among, these fanams not one is good.

Prepositions governing the ablative ഇൽ.

പിന്നെ *after*, as അതിൽപിന്നെ after that; but when it follows a verb the latter is put in the neuter participle, and should end in ഇൽ as വന്നതിൽപിന്നെ after he came; ഇതു ചെയ്തതിൽപിന്നെ after he had done this.

നിന്നു, *from*, always require the abl. in ഇൽ, ഒളം *as far as*, വീട്ടിൽഒളം as far as the house.

But observe that in speaking of rational beings, by way of comparison, this preposition will govern an accusative case, as അവനെയൊളം ദുഷ്ടനാരുമില്ല no one is so wicked as he.

Of the Ablative ഒട

1st. verbs of the following significations; of speaking, demanding, enquiring, taking at interest, fighting, of being at peace, of disputing, conquering, asking, will have the ablative in ഒട as, പറയുന്നു to speak, ചൊല്ലുന്നു to say, ചൊദിക്കുന്നു, or ചൊദിക്കുന്നു to enquire, ഉത്തരംപറയുന്നു to answer, വാങ്ങുന്നു or മേടിക്കുന്നു to receive; കൊള്ളുന്നു to buy, പിണങ്ങുന്നു to quarrel, പടവെട്ടുന്നു to fight, രമിക്കുന്നു to be appeased, തർക്കിക്കുന്നു to dispute, ജയിക്കുന്നു to conquer, തൊൽക്കുന്നു to be vanquished, അപേക്ഷിക്കുന്നു to ask, all require

require an ablative of the person in ഓട.

2dly. Also verbs of borrowing, and taking at interest പലിശക്കുവാങ്ങുന്നു I take at interest: കടംകൊള്ളുന്നു I am taking a loan.

3dly. The following verbs govern the same ablative, എതിൎക്കുന്നു, or എതിരിടുക്കുന്നു to be opposite, or adverse; ഒക്കുന്നു to be equal, ഒപ്പിക്കുന്നു to make equal, പറഞ്ഞൊക്കുന്നു to promise; സമംആകുന്നു to be equal, or ആക്കുന്നു to make equal കൂടുന്നു to be together; വെൎപ്പെടുന്നു, or വെൎപിരിയുന്നു, or വെൎതിരിയുന്നു to be separated; കളിക്കുന്നു to play; and a few other verbs, similar in sense to these.

Prepositions requiring the Ablative in ഓട,

കൂടെ, or കൂട്ടെ together with; as എന്നൊടകൂടെവന്നു he came with me; എതിരെ against, as, വിശ്വാസത്തൊടെതിരെ contrary to belief, രാജാവൊടെതിരെ against the Raja.

Of the Ablative in ആൽ,

This is used to express the mode, or cause or instrument by which any thing is done, എന്നാൽകാൎയ്യംസാധിക്കാ you will not gain your cause by my means, ദ്രവ്യത്താൽവലിപ്പംഉണ്ടാകുന്നു by riches you will achieve greatness.

It is better to express this form of speech by കൊണ്ടു, as വാളാൽ, or വാൾകൊണ്ടുമരിച്ചു he died by the sword.

Of the 4th Ablative ഇൽനിന്നു,

This form of the ablative signifies from, as എവിടെനിന്നു, or എവിടുന്നുവരുന്നു whence do you come? വീട്ടിൽനിന്നുവരുന്നു I come from home.

Sometimes

Sometimes instead of നിന്നു, they only write ന്നു, as എവിടെ ന്നു, ഇവിടെന്നു whence, hence; വീട്ടിന്നു from home, കൊച്ചിന്നു from Cochin, നഗരിന്നു from the city.

Of Adverbs.

വിശേഷിച്ച്, or വിശേഷിച്ചായ്‌ besides, or principally, എന്നാലും but, എന്നിട്ടും netherthesess, എന്നാറെ after it was so, or it having happened, എന്നതിനെക്കൊണ്ടു, or ഇതിനെക്കൊണ്ടു therefore, എങ്കിലും either, or although.

Interrogative adverbs.

എന്തെ why, എന്ത what, എന്തായി or എന്തായിട്ട why? എന്ത, or എന്തുകൊണ്ടു for what reason? അല്ലയൊ can it not? ഇല്ലയൊ is it not?

Observe, in this place, that, in interrogations, the noun, or verb must always terminate in ഒ, as അവൻ പൊയൊ is he gone? നീ പൊകുന്നൊ അല്ലയൊ do you go, or not? വിശ്വസിക്കുമൊ will you believe? നീ ചെയ്തതു നല്ലതൊ ആകാത്തതൊ what you have done is it good or ill? ഞാൻ അയച്ച ആൾ വന്നുവൊ is the person whom I sent returned? ഞാൻ കല്പിച്ചതു നീ ചെയ്തില്ലെ, Have you not done what I ordered you? But this peculiarity is better learnt by practice than rules.

To make an interrogative of the present tense, ന്നു is changed into ന്നൊ, or ഉ final into ഒ, and the same in the preterite, thus സ്നെഹിച്ചൊ did he love? ചെയ്തൊ did he do? and in the future, and in nouns ending in ം, this ൊ is is changed into ഓ as പോകുമോ will you go? വേണ്ടോ is it necessary? ഉത്തമമോ is it good?

In short the final letter, whatever it may be, must be joined with ഒ, but if the termination be ഞ്ഞു, whether the preterite of a verb, or a noun ഒഞ്ഞാ is added thereto, and the finals ൻ, ൽ, ൾ, are vocalized into ൊലാ, ൊള്ളാ and ൊഴാ.

Of Adverbs derived from nouns.

These are formed, sometimes, simply by putting the noun in the ablative in ആൽ, as, കരുണയാൽ, or കരുണയാലെ mercifully; സ്നേഹത്താൽ, or ാലെ lovingly. But this is not a common mode, and can only be used when the sense may be expressed by the prepositions *by*, or *with*; therefore, it would be more proper, always, to consider these words as substantives. The proper method of forming adverbs from nouns. is, by adding to the nominative case the preterite of the verb ആകുന്നു, namely, ആയി, or ആയിട്ടു for Example.

രാവ് night, രാവായി, or രാവായിട്ടു by night, nightly.

രാപ്പകലും by night, and by day; നന്ന good നന്നായിട്ടു well.

ദുഷ്ടത wickedness ദുഷ്ടതയായിട്ടു

സുഖം easiness സുഖമായി easily.

പ്രയാസം difficulty.

പ്രയാസമായി difficulty

സത്യം truth, സത്യമായിട്ടു truly

കാരകൻ essence കാരകലായിട്ട essentially

കാരുണ്യം mercy കാരുണ്യമായിട്ട.

Primitive Adverbs Affirmative.

ഉവ്വ yes; അതെ yes, or ſo; അതതന്നെ it is ſo; അത്രെതന്നെ just so, ഓം Sanſcrit.

Negative. ഇല്ല no (negation of exiſtence.) അല്ല no, (negation of eſſence, or qualites, or power;) ഇല്ലില്ല it certainly is not; അല്ലല്ല it cannot be; theſe are both quaint negatives to be diſcriminated by uſe.

ADVERBS OF PLACE.

എവിടെ where,

ഇവിടെ here,

അവിടെ there,

എവിടെക്ക whither,

ഇവിടെക്ക hither,

അവിടെക്ക thither,

എവിടെന്ന whence,

ഇവിടന്ന hence,

അവിടെന്ന thence,

എങ്ങും ഒരെടത്തും nowhere,

കീഴ്, or കീഴെ below,

എങ്ങ where, on which ſide,

ഇങ്ങ on this ſide ,

അങ്ങ there, on that ſide,

എങ്ങോട്ട to which ſide,

എങ്ങാനും any where,

ഇങ്ങോട്ട hither,

അങ്ങോട്ട to that ſide,

എല്ലാടത്തും every where,

മെല്, or മെലെ, and മീതെ above,

ഇതിലൂടെ this way,

അതിലൂടെ that way, (theſe not much in uſe,)

വല്ലെടത്തും any, or ſome wehre,

അടുക്കെ, അരികെ near,

ദൂരെ, ദൂരത്ത far off,

കൊല്ലപ്പുംദൂരെ very far,

മെല്പട്ട, മെല്പൊട്ട upwards,

കിഴ്പട്ട, കിഴ്പൊട്ട downwards,

മെല്ക്കുമെല് above and above,

അകം, അകത്ത within,

അകത്തൂട in ſide,

പുറത്ത without,

പുറത്തൂട out ſide,

വലത്തഭാഗത്ത to the right,

ഇടത്തഭാഗത്ത to the left,

കിഴക്കൊട്ട Eaſtward,

തെക്കൊട്ട Sonthwatd,

വടക്കൊട്ട Notthward,

പടിഞ്ഞാറൊട്ട Weſtward,

കിഴക്കതെക്കൊട്ടെക്ക South Eaſt,

വടക്കുപടിഞ്ഞാറായിട്ടു North West,

ADVERBS OF TIME.

എപ്പൊൾ when,

ഇപ്പൊൾ now,

അപ്പൊൾ then,

എപ്പൊഴും, എല്ലാപ്പൊഴും always,

ഇപ്പൊഴും, ഇന്നു even now,

അപ്പൊഴും, അന്നു even then,

എപ്പൊഴെക്ക at what time,

എന്നു when? what day?

ഇന്നു today,

അന്നു then, that day,

എന്നെക്കും, എന്നെന്നെക്കും എന്നെന്നെക്കുംകായിട്ടു always for ever,

ഇന്നലെ yesterday,

മിനിഞ്ഞാന്നു the day before yesterday,

തലെന്നാൾ the day before,

നാളെ tomorrow,

മററന്നാളെ the day after tomorrow,

പിററന്നാളെ the next day,

നാൾതൊറും, ദിനംദിനം, or ദിവസംതൊറും every day,

എല്ലാനാളും in all days,

എല്ലാനെരത്ത at all times,

മുന്നെ, മുമ്പെ at first,

പിന്നെ, പിമ്പെ afterwards,

അനന്തരം, അനന്തരം afterwards,

കിഴിൽ of old times, formerly,

അനാദിതൊട്ട from eternity,

അന്നതൊട്ടഇന്നയോളവും from that time till now,

പണ്ടെ, പണ്ട of old, formerly,

പണ്ടകാലങ്ങളിൽ in ancient times,

പൂൎവ്വത്തിങ്കൽ, or പൂൎവ്വകാലത്തിൽ in the beginning,

നടെ formerly,

കഴിഞ്ഞതിൽ in times past,

കഴിഞ്ഞാണ്ടിൽ last year,

മേലിൽ, or മേലാലെക്ക hereafter, in future,

ഇനി, or ഇനിയും from this time,

ഇനിഒരുനാളും never after this,

ഒരുനാളും never,

ഓളം, ഓളമെക്ക until,

ആണ്ടതൊറും, കാലംതൊറും every year,

വീണ്ടു, പിന്നെ again,

കാലത്താലെ, രാവിലെ early, in the morning,

ഉച്ചെക്ക at noon,

സന്ധ്യക്ക, അന്തിക്ക, വൈകിട്ട, വൈകിട്ട in the evening,

രാവിരുട്ട, രാക്കാലത്തിങ്കൽ at night,

പകൽനേരത്ത by day,

പാതിരാക്ക, പാതിരാത്രി at midnight,

ഒരിക്കൽ once,

പുലൎകാലെ very early, at day break,

നാ

നാഴികതൊറും, നാഴികകളിലും every hour,

വിനാഴികതൊറും, or എല്ലാവിനാഴികയിൽ, or വിനാഴികകളിലും every instant,

നെരംവെളുക്കുംപൊഴുത at dawn of day,

ഉദയത്തിങ്കൽ, ഉദയകാലത്തിങ്കൽ at sun rise,

സന്ധ്യാകാലത്തിങ്കൽ towards evening,

പണ്ടുകാലത്ത of old,

പുതുതായിട്ട lately, newly,

മുറുക, മുറുകവെ, തെരുതെരെ, തെരുക്കവെ, വെഗം ശീഘ്രം ക്ഷണനെരത്ത quickly, in hast especially, instantly,

കടുക്കവെ, പെട്ടന്നുക്കവെ, പെട്ടനെ, unexpectedly, suddenly,

ഉടൻ, ഉടൻതന്നെ immediately,

പതുക്ക പതുക്കെ by little and little, slowly,

മെല്ലെ, മെല്ലെ by degrees, slowly,

(In the interior parts they say പയ്യെ.പയ്യെ by degrees)

ADVERBS OF MODE &c.

കൂടെ (കൂടവെ In poetry) together,

തന്നെ exactly,

ഒന്നിച്ച jointly,

തിരിച്ച distinctly,

വെവ്വെറെ separately,

വെറുതെ, പഴുതെ, ബലാൽ, വിഫലം wantonly,

കൊറെ, കുറെശ, അല്പം, ഇത്തിരി, ഇശ്ശിരി, ഇമ്മിരി, a little,

എത്ര how much, how great; ഇത്ര

ഇത്ര ſo many, ſo much,

എത്രകുറി, എത്രഊഴം, എത്രവട്ടം how often,

എത്രൊളം, എത്രപ്പൊഴം how far,

ഇത്രപ്പൊഴം, ഇത്രൊളം ſo far,

ആവൊളം as far as poſſible

ആവൊളമൊക്ക Idem,

എറെ more, much.

എററം very much,

അത്ര only as much,

വഷളെ baſely,

ഇത്രൊട by this means,

സാക്ഷാൽ, clearly, evidently,

പക്ഷെ perhaps,

ക്രമെണക്രമംകൊണ്ടുക്രമമായിട്ട in order, regularly,

ശ്രെഷ്ഠം, ശിക്ഷ excellently, very well,

അഴകായിട്ട handſomely,

ഒട്ടൊട്ട in ſome meaſure, a little,

വെളിച്ചെ clearly,

രഹസ്യമായിട്ട, ഒളിപ്പാരലെ, ഒളിച്ചിട mysteriouſly, obſcurely, hiddenly,

പരസ്യമായി publicly,

എകദെശം for the moſt part,

Obſerve that the adverb of ſimilitude, വണ്ണം *as*, is joined to the preterite, and future participles ചെയ്തവണ്ണം as he did, പറയുംവണ്ണം as he will ſay.

This

This is sufficient on the subject of adverbs; but, whenever one is required, by adding to a noun the word ആയി, or ആയിട്ട് you will have as many adverbs as there are nouns in the language.

OF CONJUNCTIONS *between nouns.*

When there are in a sentence several nouns, they are connected with each other, by the ഉം, annexed to the end of the noun, having the power of *and*, thus, ആകാശവും ഭൂമിയും അഗ്നിയും വായുക്കളും കടലും തമ്പുരാൻ സൃഷ്ടിച്ചു God created the heaven, and the Earth, and fire, and the winds, and the sea; തമ്പുരാനും മാനുഷനും, God, and man; കാരുണ്യവും ന്യായവും mercy, and justice; കെട്ടിയവനും കെട്ടിയവളും the husband, and wife, or more elegantly ഭർത്താവും ഭാര്യയും.

This particle ഉം is also equivalent to *as well as*, and *both*, E. G. as well wisdom, as power, is conspicuous in what God hath created തമ്പുരാൻ സൃഷ്ടിച്ചതിൽ ഐശ്വര്യജ്ഞാനവും വൈശക്തിയും പ്രകാശിക്കുന്നു.

But if ഉം be added to only one noun, then it signifies *also*; അവനും ക്ഷമിക്കേണം he also ought to be pardoned: These however are more frequently expressed by adding കൂടെ, as എനിക്കും കൂടെ താ give to me also; ഞാനും കൂടെ ഉണ്ടായി I also was present.

If a negative follow, it means *neither* as പാലും ഇല്ല വെള്ളവും ഇല്ല there is neither milk nor water; ഒരുത്തനും ഇല്ല

[illegible] there is neither vice, nor virtue.

Obſerve that the conjunctions *both*, *nor*, *neither*, *alſo*, are expreſſed by the pronoun [illegible] taken adverbially, as [illegible] whether angel, or devil, or man, as well ruler, as ſubject, or ſlave, both learned and illiterate, all muſt meet together at the laſt Judgment.

Disjunctives are expreſſed by എങ്കിലും, which in this caſe ſignifies *either*, *or*; thus, either to ſuffer, or to die [illegible]; either you, or I muſt infallibly die [illegible]; giving to me either a horſe, or an ox is enough [illegible].

This ſenſe is ſometimes thus expreſſed, [illegible] either go, if not I will kill you; [illegible] In one caſe, or alternative, give me ten fanams, if you will not do that you muſt give me back my ſtag.

Of Conjunctions between Verbs.

To avoid errors, a beginner when he finds two, or three verbs in a ſentence, ſhould place all but the laſt in the preter-tenſe, and this laſt in the tenſe which the ſentence requires, E. G. He, having received money, went to Cochin, and bought

bought me new Shoes അവൻപണംഒടുക്കികൊടുത്തുകപ്പെ രയിൽപുതുക്കൻചെരിപ്പുഎനിക്കുകൊണ്ടു; He laboring, and ſweating ſupports himſelf അവൻഅദ്ധ്വാനിച്ചു വിയർത്തുപൊ റുക്കുന്നു But ſometimes verbs are connected by the particle ഉം as, ചത്തുംകെട്ടുപോയി he died, and rotted.

Alſo the neuter participles are uſed connected by the particle ഉം as, ചെയ്യുന്നതുംപറയുന്നതുംവിചാരിച്ചുസൂക്ഷിക്കേണം you muſt be careful what you do, and ſay; ചെയ്തതുംപറഞ്ഞതുംനിരൂപിച്ചതുംവെവ്വേറെകുംബസാരിക്കേണം you muſt diſtinctly confeſs what you have done, and ſaid, and thought.

Sometimes കൊണ്ടു is added to this form of ſpeech; ചെയ്തതുംപറഞ്ഞതും കൊണ്ടെനിക്കവലിയക്ലേശം ഉണ്ടു I have great concern at what I have done, and ſaid.

But when many verbs come together it is common to expreſs the connection by giving them the termination കയും, as in the caſe where they precede the reflectives ഇടും; or വെക്കും, and annexing ചെയ്യുന്നു, in the ſame manner, as before obſerved of the ornamental, or emphatic verbs. as മിശിഹാ നമുക്കവേണ്ടിദാഹിക്കയുംവിശക്കയുംദുഃഖിക്കയും കരകയുംഒടുക്കംമരിക്കയുംചെയ്തു Chriſt, for our ſakes, thirſted, and hungered, and was ſorrowful, and wept, and at length died for us.

Obſerve that interrogatives, ſome times, make disjunctions when ഒ is repeated, as ഞാനൊനീയൊ I, or you? ഇവനൊ

അവ

അവനൊ this, or that man? തിന്മാനൊ കുടിപ്പാനൊ do you wish to eat or to drink.

But, it is to be obſerved that, all nouns ending in ം have, in conjunction, the termination വും, as ആകാശവും ഭൂമിയും അതിൽ പെട്ടതൊക്കെയും തമ്പുരാൻ സൃഷ്ടിച്ചുണ്ടാക്കി God made the heaven, and the earth, and all things which are therein.

All nouns in ഈ long take the termination യും, as പാപയും തിന്മയും നന്മയും ſin, and evil, and goodneſs, from പാപ, തിന്മ, നന്മ; alſo nouns in ഇ, as, തീയും പള്ളിയും പുലിയും fire, and the Church, and a Tyger.

Nouns in എ (which is the final of almoſt all accuſative caſes,) take alſo യും, as അവനെയും അവരെയും him, and them; വൃക്ഷത്തെയും മരത്തെയും ചൊല്ലിയാലും ശരി വൃക്ഷം and മരം (names for a tree) may be uſed indifferently.

Nouns ending in ഉ add വും, as വസ്തുവും ശത്രുവും the thing, and the Enemy.

All other nouns change the vocal conſonant into ഉം as, വില്ലും നാടും മീനും തേനും വേരും പേരും ആളും കടലും കീഴും the bow, and the country, and the fiſh, and honey, and the root, and the name, and the perſon, and the ſea, and that which is beneath it.

Here it may be ſeen that, ൽ is changed into ലും, ൾ into ളും, ൻ into നും, ർ into രും, and ഴ into ഴും.

Of

Of the Particle എന്നു.

This was before obſerved to mark the infinitive mood.

It is alſo uſed 2dly. inſtead of the verb ആകുന്നു thus, അവൻ ഇതു സത്യം എന്നു പറഞ്ഞു he ſaid this was true; and, in this ſenſe it has three preterites എന്നുൻ, എന്നിട്ടു, എന്നുനെ and a participle എന്നക

Thirdly it ſeems to ſignify alſo, that is to ſay, truly &c നിന്റെ പേർ എന്തെന്നു what is your name? പേത്രു എന്നു. Peter forſooth, or ക്ലെമെന്ത് എന്നു, Clement truly, but in this ſenſe it is uſed for ആകുന്നു

Fourthly the particle എന്നു ſignifies when, and എന്നും. always.

On the Malabar Syntax.

There are not many Rules of conſtruction in the Malabar language, which have not already been laid down in the preceding pages; but, that nothing may be wanting, which the forms of grammar require, a few remarks are ſubjoined on the peculiarities of conſtruction, which are neceſſary to be learned.

This, like all other languages, has three Genders, the Maſculine, feminine, & neuter, altho the distribution of nouns under each claſs is different.

The Maſculine, പുല്ലിംഗം comprises all nouns expreſſing the names of God, Demons, and men.

The feminine സ്ത്രീലിംഗം, is confined to Goddeſſes, and women.

And

And the names of animals, trees, minerals, stars, virtues, vices, in ſhort all nouns expreſſing irrational things, are of the neuter gender, which is called നപുംസകലിംഗം.

All adjectives in this language are indeclinable, and are placed before their ſubſtantives.

All verbs have the ſame termination of the preſent tenſe, and have no variation of perſon, and, with the exception of a few irregulars, may be reduced under the form of one conjugation, in every mood, and tenſe; for which ſee the lecture on verbs.

In strictneſs of ſpeaking, there are no more than three tenſes, the preſent, the preterite, and the future, called reſpectively നില്ക്കുന്നകാലം, കഴിഞ്ഞകാലം, and വരുവാനിരിക്കുന്നകാലം, the other tenſes are ſupplied by the aid of certain prepoſitions, or particles annexed.

The following obſervations will be found very uſeful for the attainment of a thorough knowledge of the nature of the verb.

Firſt, The Malabars, ſometimes, uſe the future for the preſent, or preterite, as, അവൻമരിപ്പാൻതുടങ്ങുംപൊൾതന്റെ നല്ലമാതാവിനൊടയാത്രംചൊല്ലി when he was about to die he bade farewell to his dear mother.

The imperative alſo is uſed for the noun, as അവൻപറ കകൊണ്ടെഞാൻചതിക്കപ്പെട്ടു I was deceived by his words. The neuter participles of verbs are alſo uſed in this ſenſe

ſenſe as, നിവന്നതകൊണ്ടെനിക്കചെതംവന്നു I ſuſtained a loſs by your coming.

Secondly, It is a moſt general, and elegant practice to uſe the neuter participles of verbs, ending in ന്നത, for the preſent tenſe, or the preterite, and it is the only way of expreſſing our relative, *who* or *what*, as ഞാൻപറഞ്ഞതകെട്ടൊ did you hear what I ſaid? ഞാനവളെവളരെസ്നെഹിച്ചത I loved her exceedingly: this is peculiarly adapted to interrogations: നിന്നെസൃഷ്ടിച്ചതാര who created you? നിന്നെപഠിപ്പിച്ചതാര് who taught you? But obſerve that, to uſe this mode of expreſſion, ആര് muſt always ſtand laſt in the ſentence; for, if ആര് be placed in the beginning, the verb will be in the preterite, as ആര്നിന്നെസൃഷ്ടിച്ചു who created you? ആര്നിന്നെപഠിപ്പിച്ചു who taught you?

Thirdly, It is uſual, in common language, to uſe the termination ലെ placing the verb in the preterite, and adding thereto ഇരിക്കലെ, thus ഞാൻപറഞ്ഞിരിക്കലെ when I was ſpeaking, ഞാൻചെയ്തിരിക്കലെ while I was doing, അവിടെഇരിക്കലെ while I was there, അതചെയ്തിരിക്കലെ when I was doing it; and, in this ſenſe, correſponds with the particle പൊഴ, which is in the ſame manner ſubjoined to verbs.

The particles ങ്കിൽ; ങ്കിലും are, alſo, in a ſimilar manner, thus expreſſed by the Malabars; അതചെയ്തങ്കിൽ നിന്നെതല്ലും if you do ſo I will beat you, inſtead of ſaying അതുചെയ്യുമെങ്കിൽ; സ്നെഹിക്കിൽചെതംവ

രും

ണം, instead of saying സ്നേഹിച്ചാൽ, by loving women you will suffer ill.

Instead of എങ്കിലും they have the following mode, നീ തല്ലിയാലും ഞാൻ ചെയ്യും I will do it tho' you beat me; ചേതം വരികിലും ഞാൻ കൊള്ളും I will buy it tho' I lose; it is derived from the preterite in ാൽ, by adding ഉം, as ദുഷ്ടന്മാരെങ്കിലും നാം രാജാക്കളെ കൊല്ലുവാൻ വഹിയാ although, kings should be bad men we must not, can not kill them; അവനെ ശിക്ഷിച്ചാലും ഫലിക്കില്ല it will have no effect though you correct him.

Fourthly. Verbs in ഊ long require to be preceded by a noun ending in ഏ; such are ആവൂ, ടക്കിയാവൂ, കഴിവൂ, സ്നേഹിപ്പൂ, ഉള്ളൂ; thus, ഇതെ ആവൂ only this; the verb ആവൂ may be annexed to all verbs, as ഇത എഴുതിയെ തിന്നാവൂ you shall only eat after you have written this; അവനെ കൊന്നെ കഴിവൂ the business will be finished only after he is killed; ദുഷ്ടന്മാൎക്ക ശിക്ഷ കല്പിച്ചേ ടക്കിയാവൂ it is necessary to award punishment to evil doers.

Here it is observable that ടക്കിയാവൂം implies a necessity, as does കഴിവൂ, so എന്നെ സഹായിച്ചേ കഴിവൂ you must assist me.

Sometimes only the distant words in the sentence take this termination ഏ, the intermediate ones between these, and the verb, preserving their natural final sounds, as കാര്യം നന്നായി വിചാരിച്ചേ ഞാൻ നിന്നെ വന്നു കണ്ടെ രാജം ഞാൻ ...ക്കൂട after

ter well considering a thing you can alone determine what is right, or wrong; ഗുണംചെയ്യുന്നല്ലവൎക്കംന്യായക ളിഷ്ടി ഈശ്വരൻസ്വൎഗ്ഗലൊകസുഖംകിട്ടിയുണ്ടം It is only by doing good that you can acquire the celestial happiness, which God has promised to the virtuous.

In speaking to men of superior rank, or dignity we cannot use കൊള്ളാം but, rather, വെണം, and the antecedent verb must be in the imperative.

Thus, *be pleased to do this*, if rendered by കാൎയ്യങ്ങളെചെയ്യകൊള്ളാം, or കാൎയ്യംചെയ്യണം, implies an obligation, or necessity of doing so; it is more submissive, therefore, and respectful, to say കാൎയ്യങ്ങളെചെയ്യുവെണം.

Be pleased to go to Cochin on account of my business എ ന്റെകാൎയ്യംവെണ്ടികൊച്ചിക്കുപൊകവെണം.

Finally observe that the Malabars, sometimes, use verbs ending in ഈൎ for the optative; ഒരുനിധികിട്ടിയാൎ I wish I might find a treasure. Bnt this mode is nearly obsolete.

Also that, the verb ഉള്ളു, *it is only*, requires the preceding noun, or verb to end in എ, as ഞാൻഇതുപറഞ്ഞെഉള്ളു I only said this; ഒരിക്കൽചെയ്തെഉള്ളു I only did it once.

Fifthly, The verb തുടങ്ങുന്നു, *to begin*, requires a supine to precede it, as അവൻപ്രാൎത്ഥിപ്പാൻതുടങ്ങുന്നു he begins to pray; but frequently it has a preterite participle before it, as ന്നവ

ഞാൻ കണ്ടപ്പൊൾ ചിരിപ്പാൻ തുടങ്ങി when I saw him I began to laugh; പണിക്കു തുടങ്ങി he began to work.

Sixthly, The Malabars, by way of ornament, add ആയി, or ആയിട്ടു to supines, as അവൻ കൂടെ പൊവാനായിട്ടു ആളുകളെ വിളിച്ചു he called his people to depart; പഠിപ്പാനായിട്ടു വന്നു he came to learn; സന്തൊഷിപ്പാനായിട്ടു വീണ വരുത്തി he caused a Guitar to be brought to amuse him.

But, when there are several supines they are connected by the conjunction ഉം, and to the last so ending is added ആയിട്ടു, as തിന്മാനും കുടിപ്പാനും കളിപ്പാനും ആയിട്ടല്ല ഇവിടെ വന്നതു I am not come here to eat, and to drink, and to be merry.

There are also certain adverbs which have various influence on the verbs to which they are joined.

ഒളം *until*, requires a supine, and is added to them by taking away the final ൻ, as അവൻ വരുവൊളം പാർക്കെണം you must wait till he comes; മരിപ്പൊളം നന്മ ചെയ്യെണം we must do good till death.

മുമ്പിൽ takes before it the future, as ഉറങ്ങുവാൻ പൊകും മുമ്പിൽ ജപിക്കെണം before going to sleep we must pray.

പിന്നെ *after* requires a neuter preterite participle in the ablative in ഇൽ, as പൊയതിൽപിന്നെ after he was gone; തിന്നതിൽപിന്നെ after he had eaten.

വണ്ണം, പൊലെ *as like*, require the participle of the preterite,

terite, or future, as നീപറഞ്ഞവണ്ണംചെയ്തു I did as you told me; നീചെയ്യുംപൊലെഞാൻചെയ്യും I will do as you shall do.

ഒക്കവണ്ണം, ഒത്തവണ്ണം, ഒക്കപൊലെ, *according to*, require the neuter participle in the dative as നീകല്പിച്ചതിനൊടൊത്തവണ്ണംചെയ്തു I did according to what you ordered.

ശെഷം *after*, takes the neuter participle preterite in the genitive, വന്നതിന്റെശെഷം after he was come, പൊയതിന്റെശെഷം after he departed.

There are also two adverbs താനും, and പൊല്ലൊ which confer great elegance, and energy on verbs to which they are added, though of themselves they have no sense. It may however appear that താനും signifies, but, and പൊല്ലൊ truly, namely, വളരെവിഷമമുണ്ടായിക്കാര്യംസാധിച്ചുതാനും I had great difficulty but I accomplished the business, അവനിവിടെവന്നുപൊല്ലൊ he came indeed hither.

Seventhly, We proceed to a few remarks on the irregular verbs; വെണം, ഏണം, അരുത, as before observed, require the preceding verb to end in യും; the same happens, sometimes, to വെണ്ട I will not; വായിക്കകയുംഎഴുതുകയുംവെണം പറികയുംവെണ്ട you must read, and write, you must not speak.

The verb വെണം has വെണ്ടു in the preterite, which is frequently joined in common discourse with the imperative terminating in ൻ, and thus signifies permission to do a thing

as,

ക, പോകവേണ്ടു you may go; ഇരിക്കവേണ്ടു you may sit തല്ലവേണ്ടു strike.

From the verb വേണ്ടു is derived വേണ്ടില്ല it is not necessary, or വേണ്ടുകയില്ല; and വേണ്ടില്ലാഞ്ഞു it was not necessary. participle വേണ്ടാത്ത, or വേണ്ടില്ലാത്ത; വേണ്ടില്ലാഞ്ഞാൽ if it be not necessary; വേണ്ടില്ലെങ്കിലും altho' it be useless.

The verb പോകാ is added to the preterite of other verbs, and has the power of *I know not*; as ചെയ്യപ്പോകാ I know not how to do it പറയപ്പോകാ I cannot speak.

പോകും, joined to preterites and signifies *to know to be able* as പറഞ്ഞുപോകും I know, അറിഞ്ഞുപോകും I can speak; അറിഞ്ഞുപോകുന്നവൻ a learned men അറിഞ്ഞുപോകാത്തവൻ with the negative *a* long, an ignorant man.

Sometimes പോകും takes an imperative before it, as അവൻ ഇതുഉണ്ടാക്കപോകുമൊ will he know how to do it.

ആവതില്ല I am unable, pret. ആവതില്ലാഞ്ഞു; this verb requires a dative case.

വശമല്ല, or വശമില്ല I cannot; വശമില്ലാഞ്ഞു, വശമില്ലാഞ്ഞു; the other tenses like ഇല്ലാ; subs: വശമില്ലാഞ്ഞാൽ; this verb takes before it a dative of the person, and the supines of verbs വേലചെയ്‌വാൻവശമില്ലാ I cannot work.

പോരും, which signifies any thing dubious, or which may take place, requires before it a supine ending in ഉം, thus അവനെ ദീനം ഭേദിപ്പാനും പോരും perhaps he may recover from his infirmties; ഇതു ഉണ്ടാകുവാനും പോ

പൊരും It may be there will be a war this year.

പൊരാ *it is not enough*, when joined to a verb, requires the preterite in ആൽ, as, നീ ഈകാൎയ്യത്തെചെയ്യാഞ്ഞാൽ പൊരാ മൊക്ഷത്തിൽപൊകവാൻനല്ലതുകൂടെപ്രവൃത്തിക്കെണം. It is not enough that you do not ill, to obtain glory you must also do good; സ്വാമിയെ സ്വാമിയെ കൎത്താവെ വിളിച്ചാൽപൊരാമൊക്ഷംകിട്ടുവാൻഗുണംകൂടെചെയ്യുകയുംവെണ്ടൂ It is not sufficient to say Lord, Lord, and master, to gain heaven; you must likewise practise virtue.

ഉണ്ട is sometimes placed before verbs without any particular meaning, as അവൻ ഉണ്ടൊവരുന്നു Is he coming? instead of saying അവൻവരുന്നൊ; നീ ഉണ്ടൊ ഇതചെയ്തു have you done this, for നീഇതചെയ്തിട്ടുണ്ടൊ.

Two negatives, in the Malabar language, do not make an affirmative, therefore if there be a negative noun the verb it governs should be also negative, thus ആരും വന്നിട്ടില്ലാ no one came, ഒരുത്തനും കണ്ടിട്ടില്ല I saw no one; നിങ്ങൾകണ്ട കാഴ്ച ഒരുത്തനൊടും പറയരുത the vision which ye saw tell to no one.

Sometimes ഉണ്ട is used after വെണം, and then expresses ഇഷ്ടതി *in need of* as ഇത്രവെഗംവെണമെന്നഉണ്ടൊ is so much hurry necessary? വെണമെന്നഉണ്ട it is necessary.

They use also, with elegance, ഇല്ല, after വെണമെന്ന, or വെണമെന്നകാൽ, as, മൊക്ഷംനെടുവാൻഇപ്പൊഴ്തന്നെ നല്ലനടക്കണമെന്നില്ല, or നല്ലനടക്കണമെന്നകാലിൽ ഇല്ല

ല്ല to acquire bliss it is not necessary always to fast; അതുവെണ്ടുന്നില്ല there is no need for that; ഇതുവിശ്വസിക്കെണമെന്നു നിർബന്ധമില്ല it is not absolutely necessary to believe this.

When two verbs come together, in a sentence, even of opposite meaning, the former is always in in the preterite tense; as പൊയിട്ടുവന്നു I went, and came; പൊയിട്ടുവരുമ്പൊൾ when I shall have gone and come.

The genitive is placed first of two nouns, in whatever case they may be; the noun before the verb, and this latter always at the end of the sentence.

When many verbs meet together in a sentence, all the former are put in the preterite participle; the last, only, in that tense which the context requires. E. G. Fear God, pray daily, eschew sin, practice virtue, repent for sins committed, and thus ye will save your souls തമ്പുരാനെ പെടിച്ചു നിത്യം പ്രാർത്ഥിച്ചു ദൊഷങ്ങളെ ഉപെക്ഷിച്ചു പുണ്യങ്ങളെ പ്രവൃത്തിച്ചു ചെയ്ത ദൊഷങ്ങളെക്കുറിച്ചു മനസ്താപപ്പെട്ടു ഇങ്ങിനെ നിങ്ങളുടെ ആത്മാക്കളെ രക്ഷിക്കും

Here, all the antecedent verbs are in the preterite participle; the last, only, in the imperative.

LECTURE TWELTH,

ON THE ORTHOGRAPHY.

It is not enough to be able to speak any language, it is also necessary

necessary to know how to write with correctness the ideas you would express; for in this respect, principally, the line may be drawn between the learned, and the vulgar. I shall therefore proceed to lay down a few rules of strict orthography in the language; by attending to which, beginners may be guided in writing, and considerably assisted in reading Malabar compositions.

First, Whenever a vowel at the end of a word is followed by one of the same sort in the beginning of another, the final vowel, or more properly the initial is cut off; or absorbed in the preceding, thus, വിശ്വാസത്തിന്നടാത്തവസ്തു a thing contrary to belief, from വിശ്വാസത്തിന്ന and അടാത്ത where the initial അ of അടാത്ത is struck out; പുലിവിടെഉണ്ടു here is a tyger, from പുലിഇവിടെ &c. പള്ളിക്കിപ്പോൾപൂട്ടിയിരിക്കുന്നു the Church is now shut, from പള്ളിക്കഇപ്പോൾപൂട്ടി and ഇരിക്കുന്നു; ശത്രൂപദ്രവം for ശത്രു and ഉപദ്രവം the annoyance of an Enemy; അവരെല്ലാവരെയുംകൊന്നു he slew them all, for അവരെ and എല്ലാവരെയും; എന്നാലൊത്തതുതരുമൊ will you then give me what you promised? for എന്നാലെ, and ഒത്തത്.

Secondly, observe that, if the short *a* united to any consonant be followed by a ഊ long, instead of the latter they use the mark, called [illegible]; thus. ാ after the former as വന്നാവ the person who came, for വന്നഊവ; പോയവകാര who went for പോയഊവകാര; so also രണ്ടാണ്ടായി it is already two years, from രണ്ടഊണ്ടഊയി.

But

But if the sign of ഉ്ചം be followed by a long ഈ, the latter is cut off, thus പടയായപ്പോൾ when it was war, from പടഈയായപ്പോൾ; as is also the case when the *a* short comes in the last place, അമ്മെവിടെഉണ്ടൊ is your mother there? from അമ്മെ (for അമ്മ) and അവിടെഉണ്ടൊ.

Thirdly, that if അ short be followed by either of these letters, ഇന്ന, ഉ, ഈ, ഒ, or ഓ, the final അ takes the found, aud nature of the following vowel. E. G. ദ്രവ്യമിപ്പോൾപണമില്ല from ദ്രവ്യമിപ്പോൾപണം ഇല്ല, I.have no money at present; വരുമൊഉണ്ടൊ will he come? from വരുംഎന്നുഉണ്ടൊ. പറഞ്ഞതുതരികവേണം you must give me what you promised, from പറഞ്ഞതുതരിക&c.

The finals ൾ ൻ ൺ ർ ൽ ൾ and ം, if followed by a vowel, change this mute letter into a vocal consonant, assuming the nature of the vowel following, thus ഇപ്പോൾസമയമില്ല I nave not time at present, from ഇപ്പോൾസമയം ഇല്ല: കണ്ടാലറിയും by feeing I shall know, from കണ്ടാൽഅറിയും; so, also എന്റെമകളിവിടെവന്നൊ is my daughter come here? from മകൾഇവിടെ; ആരിവിടെഉണ്ടു who is here? for ആർഇവിടെഉണ്ടു; ആരുമില്ല, from ആരും ഇല്ല, there is no one; തെനീച്ച a bee, from തേൻ honey, and ഈച്ച a fly.

Sometimes ൾ final is transported to the following letter, which, in this case, must be doubled and the ർ expressed by a dash written over; thus മാർപാപ്പാ, the holy Pontiff, is is written കായ്യായ്യ; and വെവ്വിട്ടു for വെൎവിട്ടു it disunited, or he detached himself; അവൎചത്തുപൊയി, they are dead, may be written അവച്ചത്തുപൊയി.

The letter ൺ is in a similar manner vocalized, with following letters; but sometimes it is united with the succeeding consonant; thus പെണ്ണുകെട്ടു, matrimony, may be written പെങ്കെട്ടു; and പെൺപൈതൽ a young girl or, പെമ്പൈതൽ, പെൺകുട്ടി; പെൺവൎഗ്ഗം is properly written പെണ്വൎഗ്ഗം the female sex.

The same takes place with the ൻ final, അവൻതന്നെ, himself, is written അവന്തന്നെ; ഞാൻതന്നെ I myself ഞാന്തന്നെ; ഉടൻതന്നെ this instant ഉടന്തന്നെ; whence arises the junction of letters, which may be seen in the alphabet, such as ന്ത ന്ദ ന്ത്യ ങ്ക &c.

The final ം is, sometimes, united with a following consonant, as if it was ൻ, thus വരുംതാനും is generally written വരുന്താനും yet he will come; ചെയ്യുംതാനും I will do ചെയ്യുന്താനും &c.

Fourthly, observe that the vowels are only used in the beginning of a word, hence if അ, or ഇ be followed by any vowel this latter is changed into വ്വ, വ്വി, വ്വു, വ്വെ, വ്വൊ, as അവ്വാൾ, that person, instead of അ ആൾ; ഇവ്വാൾ instead of ഇ ആൾ this person; ഇവ്വൂഴം instead of ഇ ഊഴം this time, or turn.

If ക or കി be found in the middle of a word, it is doubled

led, to distinguish it from ന, as ഇക്കൎമ്മം this sacrifice; കൈക്കൊള്ളുന്നു to receive, from കൈ, and കൊള്ളുന്നു.

Finally, observe that, if ൻ, or ം at the end of a word, be followed by the consonant റ, from the junction of the two is formed the double letter ന്റ, thus വരുംനെരത്ത, when he will come, write വരുന്നെരത്ത; അവൻറളവിട്ടെടുത്തു, he took the measure, is written അവന്റളവിട്ടെടുത്തു; but this is less frequent in prose than in poetry.

Whence it appears that, in order to write well, a perfect knowledge of the language is required, as well as of all the combinations of the letters, which are not few, but which may be all acquired by a desire to learn, and unremitted application.

LECTURE THIRTEENTH,

Of the principal Seasons of the year, and of life, the signs of the Zodiac, the months, days of the week, and planets.

The Malabarians know but two vicissitudes of seasons; the fair weather, and the rainy season, and which may be called their summer, and winter; the former they call വെനൽ, വെയിലുള്ളകാലം the fair, or season of sun shine; and the latter വൎഷം, or കൎക്കിടകകാലം the rainy season.

The year is called കാലം, ആണ്ട, വത്സരം, സംവത്സരം, അബ്ദം hence ഇക്കാലം, ഇയ്യാണ്ട this year; കഴിഞ്ഞകാലം, or കഴിഞ്ഞാണ്ട last year വരുന്നകാലം the ensuing year.

The

The year of one's age is called വയസ്സ.

An age is called യുഗം, of which they reckon four, anſwering to the Golden, Silver, Braſs, and Iron ages of the European mythology, which they call കൃതയുഗം, ത്രേതായുഗം, ദ്വാപരയുഗം, കലിയുഗം, Krada, Treda, Dwapara and Kali.

The Malabars compute their preſent Era from the building of the City കൊല്ലം, (Kollam) once a flouriſhing place, now called Coillao, or Quilon; thus the year 1796 correſponds to the Malabar calculation 971, and is written by them കൊല്ലംതൊള്ളായിരത്തെഴുപത്തൊന്നാംകൊല്ലം, or ൯൱൭൰൧.

Leap year is called കള്ളക്കൊല്ലം.

Thoſe who live in the Island of വൈപ്പ്, Veppi, or vaypin, compute from the time at which the ſea began to retreat from their land, and the above ſaid year will crreſpond with their date of 456, commencing the year on the firſt of ſeptember.

We reckon both from the Malabar, and Chriſtian; the latter is with us ക്രിസ്താപിറന്നു, or ആണ്ടുകൾക്കൊരായിരത്തെഴുനൂറ്റിതൊണ്ണൂറ്റാറാംകൊല്ലം one thouſand ſeven hundred and ninety ſix years after the birth of Chriſt, or according to Engliſh computation.

The months are derived from the ſigns of the Zodiac, and are as follows.

മേടം

മകരം Capricorn, is made മകരമാസം January, from this name മകരം, and മാസം; a month.

കുംഭം, or കുംടം a Pitcher (aquarius) കുംടമാസം February.

മീനം the fishes മീനമാസം March.

മെടം the ram മെടമാസം April.

ഇടവം the bull ഇടവമാസം May.

മിഥുനം the twins മിഥുനമാസം June.

കർക്കിടകം the crab കർക്കിടകമാസം July, or കർക്കടകം or കർക്കടമാസം.

സിംഹം the Lion സിംഹമാസം August, or ചിങ്ങം, or ചിങ്ങ, or ചിങ്ങമാസം.

കന്നി the Virgin, കന്നിമാസം September, or കന്ന്യ a Virgin, കന്ന്യമാസം.

തുലാം the balance തുലാമാസം October.

വൃശ്ചികം the Scorpion വൃശ്ചികമാസം November.

ധനു the Archer ധനുമാസം December, or ധനുസ്സ; idem in the Samscrit tongue.

If you add to the foregoing, instead of മാസം a word of the same signification viz. ഞായറ് you will have മകരഞായറ് the month of January; കുംടഞായറ് the month of february &c.

The month is also called തിങ്ങൾ; but this it, must be remembered, cannot be added to the signs of the zodiac.

ആഴ്ച the week is called ആഴ്ച, or ആഴ്ചവട്ടം.

The

The days of the week are taken, like the Roman, from the names of the Planets as ഞായറാഴ്ച, or ഞായറാഴ്ച sunday; തിങ്കളാഴ്ച monday; ചൊവ്വ Mars ചൊവ്വാഴ്ച Tuesday; ബുധൻ Mercury ബുധനാഴ്ച wednesday; വ്യാഴം Jupiter വ്യാഴാഴ്ച thursday; വെള്ളി Venus വെള്ളിയാഴ്ച friday; ശനി Saturn ശനിയാഴ്ച saturday,

ആഴ്ചതൊറും daily; the final ആ of this word is long, and it is declined like പട war.

The day is called ദിവസം, ദിനം, അഹസ്സ, and നാൾ tho' sometimes ആഴ്ച; but in reckoning the days of the moon's increase, or decrease the word ദിവസ is always used, and never ദിവസം, മൂന്നാം ദിവസ the third day, നാലാംദിവസ the fourth.

The word പക്കം is also used in the same sense, as എത്രാംദിവസ, or എത്രാംപക്കമാൺ how many days of the moon's age? മൂന്നാംദിവസ, or മൂന്നാംപക്കം the third day; അഞ്ചാംദിവസ, or അഞ്ചാംപക്കം the fifth day; പതിമൂന്നാംദിവസ, or പതിമൂന്നാംപക്കം the thirteenth day.

The anniversary of a person's death is called ആണ്ടുചാത്തം, ചാത്തം signifying day of death.

The day is called പകൽ in contradistinction to the night, which is called രാവ, രാത്രി, സന്ധ്യ.

A holy day പെരുനാൾ.

A Birth day is പിറന്നാൾ; of a king തിരുനാൾ.

An unlucky day is termed ദുർദ്ദിനം, or ദുർദ്ദിവസം, and ചീത്തദിവസം.

To

To obſerve the day whether lucky, or not നാളുനൊക്കുക; നാക്കനൊക്കുക.

ഞങ്ങൊവാകും ഒങ്ങളുടെ വെണ്ടുന്നതിന്നു ഉത്സാഹിച്ചിട്ടു ന്നുയകൂപനല്ലനാളുനൊക്കി ചന്ദ്രദ്വീപിലെക്ക പൊകയും ചെയ്തു the good man, who ſtrived all in his power for our ſakes, having obſerved a lucky day, went to Chandra-diva.

൯൭൫ആമതു ധനുമാസം ൩ തിയ്യതി തിങ്കളാഴ്ച്ച നാളു ശ്രീരാമസ്വാമിയുടെ തിരുനാളു ഞ്ഞകൊണ്ടു ഗണപതിയെ പ്രാർത്ഥിച്ചു ഇങ്കരിയച്ചു ടച്ചു തിരിക്ക കൊഴിക്കൊട്ടിൽ പടിപ്പുര വീട്ടിൽ പണ്ടാരം രാമസ്വാമി; it was young Pandaram Ram Swamy, of the houſe of Padipura in Calicut, who, obſerving that monday the third day of the month of Danoo of the Malabar year 975 (16th. December 1799) was the anniverſary of the birth of Ram Swamy (The Lord, and Maſter) having implored Ganabady (God of Wiſdom,) put in the laſt type that brings this firſt attempt at an Engliſh Malabar Grammar to an

END